Self-Celebration

Self-Celebration

Celebrate Yourself

Olly Sanya

BALBOA.
PRESS

A DIVISION OF HAY HOUSE

Balboa Press books may be ordered through booksellers or by contacting:

Balboa Press
A Division of Hay House
1663 Liberty Drive
Bloomington, IN 47403
www.balboapress.com
1 (877) 407-4847

Because of the dynamic nature of the Internet, any web addresses or links contained in this book may have changed since publication and may no longer be valid. The views expressed in this work are solely those of the author and do not necessarily reflect the views of the publisher, and the publisher hereby disclaims any responsibility for them.

The author of this book does not dispense medical advice or prescribe the use of any technique as a form of treatment for physical, emotional, or medical problems without the advice of a physician, either directly or indirectly. The intent of the author is only to offer information of a general nature to help you in your quest for emotional and spiritual well-being. In the event you use any of the information in this book for yourself, which is your constitutional right, the author and the publisher assume no responsibility for your actions.

Any people depicted in stock imagery provided by Thinkstock are models, and such images are being used for illustrative purposes only.
Certain stock imagery © Thinkstock.

Printed in the United States of America.

ISBN: 978-1-4525-9184-1 (sc)
ISBN: 978-1-4525-9185-8 (hc)
ISBN: 978-1-4525-9186-5 (e)

Library of Congress Control Number: 2014902262

Balboa Press rev. date: 7/29/2014

Contents

Part 3

Actions That Can Hinder Self-Celebration

Introduction

This book is for everyone and will be much appreciated by people that have worked hard in life. You will be blessed by this book if you have been through a lot. If you feel things are not going as well as they should be, you should realise that you can celebrate yourself. You are a great individual, you are very special, and your life is worth celebrating. There are so many ways you can do this on a daily basis. It is time for you to arise and become the great person that you want to be. It is time for you to know that you are not in this life to wander about but to become a success.

This book will highlight the principles you have to understand in order to be able to celebrate yourself in life. You are meant to be high in life and never down. You were made for the purpose of reaching the maximum in your life. There is nothing wrong with you; you will get to the place that you are determined to go.

Celebrating yourself has to do with your feelings and thoughts. You can feel better about yourself, and you can think better about yourself. You need to be exposed to the fact that celebrating yourself is easy. Self-celebration is about self pride, achievements, and self-esteem. Self-celebration is about singling yourself out amidst the crowd. No matter where you are in life, in the midst of people you should be able to identify yourself as a special and respected person.

You have to celebrate yourself now, and this book will help you start the wonderful journey, enabling you to build a life of happiness. Reading this book will make things clearer and will bring meaning to the difficult and trying times you are experiencing. You are not going to die. You are going to make it through the difficulties you are experiencing at the moment. You are going to achieve something special in life. You are going to be respected everywhere you go.

I have seen successful people who do not celebrate themselves every day; they simply keep on working hard, but they do not understand the power of self-celebration and its benefits. Not everyone who is successful practises the principle of self-celebration. You need to be happy about where you are in life, and it's important for you to have a positive view of yourself. That's what I call self-celebration.

We all celebrate our birthdays. Birthdays are one of

the ways of celebrating yourself, but doing celebration every day is the best. You need to keep a mind of self-celebration. You can celebrate yourself by enjoying your life to the maximum and doing things that centre around your passions, interests, motivations, joy, and happiness.

People want to have a reason to celebrate every day. You cannot just live any lifestyle and celebrate in life – you have to know the secret to celebration, and it should be intentional so that celebration can happen for you and for your benefit. I know you want to feel good about yourself and be pleased about yourself; this book will expose you to that. It will help you to fill in the missing gaps of self-celebration in your life.

There are principles that have helped shape me, and they continue to help me celebrate myself in my relationships, in my family, and in my career. I know these principles work because I have experienced them first-hand. I have tasted self-celebration and know the power that it carries; I have seen it work out for those that practise it. I know that it will work out for you too. Therefore do not joke with this book, because it will expose you to the best of your life.

A lot of people want to get by the day-to-day problems without realising that they can live a life of self-celebration. This is the time for you to set aside those difficulties and start celebrating. You can enjoy your life. You can start expecting the best for your days and looking forward to the beauty of life.

You may want to be celebrated by others; however, you don't have to wait for them before you start celebrating yourself. By the time you start practising the principles in this book, you will be on a road of self-celebration in life. This book will help you to feel better about yourself, make you judge yourself positively, and keep you aspiring for the best through your days.

The most common question is, How do I know that I am celebrating myself? To celebrate is to lift up with pride and happiness. Most people celebrate their birthdays and weddings. Remember how you felt on the day you were celebrating your birthday or wedding? You felt good. It was all about goodness. That's the same way you need to feel about yourself in order to celebrate your life.

Someone cannot simply pick up a microphone during your birthday and start talking bad about you. If that happens, you will get rid of the person. Saying bad things about you does not relate to self-celebration; therefore you have to cancel all the negative things that are going through your mind regarding yourself. You have to carry out a powerful exchange of those things for the good ones. You are a very important person, and you deserve a happy life.

In your inner being, you desire to celebrate yourself. In this book you will be able to see that your best is about to come, and the future will be very interesting for you. Your future will be filled with beauty and glorious things. You will go far beyond your imagination and thinking.

In this book I want to help you amend your thoughts towards things you experience in life. I want you to celebrate yourself to the best; always keep that in mind. I want you to start singing beautiful songs of praise in your mind. Say a big 'Well done!' to yourself for all the works that you have done. I know you will come out to become the very best when the time comes. You will surely shine in this world, and nothing is going to stop you.

I am concerned about how you feel about yourself now. This book will help you to see the good things about yourself, and it will help you make necessary adjustments in order to maintain a positive self-image. It will help you to focus on the areas of your strengths, even helping you view your weaknesses as strengths.

You have to be honest to yourself. How do you feel about yourself deep inside? If you feel good, that's great to hear.

If you feel bad, this book will help you realise that there is a lot going on that should cause you to celebrate yourself. You have to celebrate every step you take in life. You have to see that there are possibilities for you to break through, even in the smallest steps.

If you have been hearing negative voices that tell you bad things about yourself, that's about to change. In this book you will learn how to remove the bad voices and focus on the right, positive things. There is nothing bad if you wake up one morning and you feel great about yourself. However, we are all in a life of battle, and we can easily hear negative voices which can stop self-celebration. You are a winner, and you are more than a conqueror. The whole of this earth is for you, and the goodness in it is for you to enjoy and explore.

Celebrating yourself in life is essential because it will give you confidence and keep your head up, reminding you that you are a special person. You are not just in life for the sake of it – you are here to succeed and become notable in all the things you do.

You will feel blessed by the time you start learning to celebrate yourself. You will be happier, more motivated, more passionate, and highly focused. You will run your race with a free flow. You will go high and climb above the mountains. You will achieve big things, and you will have a big smile on your face. You will not fall.

You might still be waiting for others to celebrate you, but you can do it for yourself. By the time you do it and start following the principles that lead to self-celebration, you will see that others will also celebrate you and will be happy for you. They will notice something special about you and wonder about how you have made it. They will be very surprised, and they will follow you with joy.

This book will be very familiar to you because it will talk about the daily things you are going through which can hinder you from celebrating yourself. I will expatiate on these things and explain how you can change them or turn them into things that will work out to your benefit. I will teach you how to take charge of your day. In this book I will connect to you, to your strengths and weaknesses, to your good side and bad side. I will make you feel good on the inside regardless of what you may be going through.

This book will help you discover that there is a light in you, and I will give you the principles that will help you ignite the light. You are meant to be in a shining environment. You are a star that cannot be hidden. You are a grace where there is no grace. You are a solution for the world and to the problems of many.

I will also teach you how to love yourself, whether you are right or wrong. You have to know that you are on the right side and you are doing the right thing. You have to know that you have tried and have come a long way. You have to keep a positive mind regarding yourself; even when you make a mistake, see it as perfection in disguise.

Soon you will have hope in a time of no hope, and courage in a time of no courage. You are going far and are going to reach a long distance in life. You are going to do things that are great, and you are going to have a future that is sweet. You are going to achieve a great deal in your lifetime. You are going further than you ever thought possible.

In this book I have the love that you need to see you through. This book will pamper you, protect you and keep you smiling through the storms of life. It's not about what you are going through – it's about where you are going. A special person like you that is going through a little darkness will become a giant in the future. You will surely overcome your down days. You will be big and you will be known. It will be over soon, and you will be a great name in the minds of people.

Part 1

What Leads to Self-Celebration?

Your success can be guaranteed by what you open up to understand. Try to understand the meaning of self-celebration.

Chapter 1
What Is Self-Celebration?

Self-celebration can be defined as the process of feeling a sense of joy towards yourself and having contentment that you will produce the best results in different areas of your life. Self-celebration helps you see yourself as the best. We all have a way we see ourselves. Some people see themselves as great, and some see themselves as ordinary. Some people think they are able, and some feel they are unable. Some people have taken a step to achieve an extra height in life, and others are still in the position of yesterday. However, I want you to know that the most excellent things lie on the inside of you. You should be on top, and nothing should stop you. You should go for the finer things in life that will beautify you.

You do not have to hold a party to celebrate yourself; simply by having a positive view of yourself, you are already engaging in self-celebration. By seeing yourself as someone that is on top, you are already celebrating yourself.

Self-celebration is about judging yourself positively on the inside. It's about casting away all those things that make you feel like you are in your little days.

Self-celebration is standing high and standing strong. It's about knowing that you can rise to achieve something fabulous in this life. It's about getting up to realise that there is a beautiful line of glory over your life. Self-celebration awakens you to the fact that you are worth something great and that there is no point in you seeing yourself as a small person.

Self-celebration gives you a good sense of yourself and makes you feel good about yourself. Self-celebration does not just happen; it happens when you understand that you are of a high value and that your life carries a great sense of uniqueness. No matter how small the areas of your life or daily operations, you have something to do. You have one or two things that you do every day, and you have to celebrate them.

If you are already celebrating yourself, your past success is great, but you can do better. I believe you will receive a higher level of self-satisfaction by celebrating yourself every day. You will see yourself in a new way, and you will feel very fresh. By celebrating yourself, you will see that you aren't in this world by mistake; you are here because your presence makes the world a better place.

By celebrating yourself, you will see that you are a fantastic person. You will discover the inner jewels that you carry. You will see that there is no one better than you. You will love yourself more, and you will carry yourself high. You will be fascinated about the fact that you can do various things in life. You can be multi-talented and very active; you can go far, and you can see that there is a lot of gift inside of you. You are precious.

No matter where you meet yourself in life, you can celebrate and develop an excellent view of yourself. How do you see yourself amidst people? Do you think you are simply there, in the background? I believe the answer is no, because you are there for a purpose. You are an example to others. Even your appearance should tell people a lot about you: the way you dress should tell them that you are a special person and that you understand the value your life carries. Then, you can celebrate yourself.

You can celebrate yourself despite:

- Your mistakes

- Your imperfections

- Your non-achievements

- Your low level or position

- Your incompetence

- Your weaknesses

- Your bad habits

- Your imperfect relationships

- Your difficulties

- Your negative thoughts

- Your bitterness

- Your self-pity

- Your sadness

- Your self-condemnation

- Your negative self-prophecies

- Your self-criticism

You will not be able to celebrate yourself if you view your weaknesses wrongly. Your weaknesses include your imperfections and faults. If you view your weaknesses as not being able, and then you compare yourself to others; this is not good. Everyone has a weakness, and you should know that your weaknesses will become strengths one day.

You are not going to be weak forever. You should also view your weakness as a little part of your life, but celebrate the big part, which contains your strengths. You should not always look at your imperfections; instead, talk about your strengths. Viewing your weaknesses wrongly can make you hide your talent. If you are still focusing on your weak side, you will be unable to go out there and make things right. You will not be able to face others when you feel weak inside. However, realise that those you are looking at also have weaknesses. You are very special, so don't feel weak.

Unprofitable relationships are relationships that do not add value or worth to your life due to what it releases. If you are in a relationship whereby someone is speaking negative things into your life, then you have to find your way out or ensure that you do not turn to that person when you are having hard times. If you come to a person, and he or she speaks bad things about you, you will only feel bad – and feeling bad does not add happiness to yourself. Therefore, you are better off getting rid of the person. Life is about happiness. Your happiness is essential, and you have the right not to allow anything to hinder it. Instead, celebrate the good things about yourself.

In order to celebrate yourself in life, you have to keep making improvements in every area. You have to ask yourself, 'What can I do better?' You have to improve in order to be ahead of others. You have to run your race and see yourself in high places. You have to be better off than the crowd by making any little adjustment that you can. You have to pick up new skills that will be useful in making your life and your talents better and brighter.

In order to improve, you need a plan. You have to first analyse the gap between your current position and where you are heading. Then you should come up with a list of things you will do so that you can get there. You always have to dream big and think of new things that you can add to your life. You have to look up and see yourself in a place where you will have a life that will be interesting to others, a place where others will always admire you and see you as a role model. I am not saying that you have to seek people's approval. I am saying that if you celebrate yourself, others will be attracted to you automatically. You can achieve it, because there is nothing that you cannot do.

People who are on top in life and whom we all celebrate are people who seek improvement and have excellent attitudes. They are always getting better. They come up with beautiful ideas and use them to show how awesome they are. They are sharp and excellent in their ways. Their dream is to stand out, and they do all that it takes to achieve it. They are not stagnant and always give room to make changes to themselves. They face challenges and overcome them. They are not afraid at all.

You should always improve in life no matter how small the change you can bring. You should know that improvement is also a sign of excellence. Nowadays people win gold medals because they are always improving. They always want to be the best, and they want to outshine the crowd. They want their name to go high. They want to be known. You too can achieve that – nothing is impossible for you. You are not little; you are just great. You have a lot of capabilities, and you have to make use of them.

When you try to always celebrate yourself, you will have a lot of fun. You will enjoy yourself more and will be more excited about your days. I do not know what is stopping you from celebrating yourself, because I am not you. However, I urge you to overcome anything that is limiting you from celebrating yourself. I want you to have something to look forward to in your life. Be filled with energy every day that you live. See yourself as someone that has a great personality, as someone special that the world is looking forward to meeting. See yourself as someone that holds great value in the midst of others. Don't misjudge yourself or view the things that you do as something little that can't get you anywhere. Be joyful about your nature and see it as something very special and worthy. See yourself as someone that others should learn from and imitate in life. See yourself as an example no matter where you are in life.

Don't allow the threats that you have on the inside to hold you back. Do not think that others are better than you. Do not think that others deserve something but you do not. Always count yourself as someone of value in the midst of a group of people. What you have to say really matters; you are counted and not excluded. There is nothing wrong in you. You still have something precious that will make others seek you.

Make a move to celebrate yourself every day. Go far to show the world what you have. Make sure that you are shining wherever you are. Have great conversations with people about yourself and your achievements. Talk to people so that they can see the right picture of who you are. Don't give up on yourself in the area of self-celebration; there is a lot for which you can celebrate yourself. Don't hide your face in the dark, thinking that you are not worth celebrating. The change begins now, and it starts with you. You have to lead a life of self-celebration.

Give room for a shift in your life. Allow those that know you to see the difference. Let them see that you now understand what it means to celebrate yourself. Place a beautiful rose on your life and begin to think high. Think of something special that you can do. Do something beautiful and different. Allow your bad past to be over, and don't let it stop you anymore. Leave all the hurt and pain of yesterday behind and allow it to die. Move on, shine on, be glad, and have something to rejoice for. Start today to view your life as a beautiful one.

Place yourself in a position whereby you will be able to celebrate yourself. Allow the world to see you celebrating yourself. Enjoy the fact that you are celebrating every part and moment of your life. Don't feel bored, like there is nothing special going on with you. Relocate your mind from that place of feeling 'same old, same old'. There are new things waiting for you out there. Don't stay in environments that do not give room to self-celebration. Enjoy your best today and do not allow anything to stop you.

When you love yourself, you will see a miracle on the inside of yourself. Your life will be a miracle. You might be faced with so many impossibilities and limitations today, but it will not be the same tomorrow. As long as you believe in yourself and celebrate yourself, you will see a miracle, which is a great turn-around in your life. Your life will never be the same, and you will mount up with wings as eagles to fly. Eagles fly high in life and you too can. You can be extremely successful.

I hope you will meet good friends in life that will show you and describe to you how wonderful you are. Love isn't about finding a perfect person; it's about seeing an imperfect person as a perfect person. A good friend will always view you as a perfect person and will be a source of strength to you. The friend will celebrate your life with you and will stay beside you. Love heals everything. A good friend will show you love that will go a long way in healing you from hurt. That friend will hold you up and will spread good things upon your heart.

Your good friends will always value you. They enjoy what is on the inside of you. They like the way they feel when they are with you. They know what they are able to achieve using your presence. They see you as far better and braver than you think you are. Therefore, you don't have to be shy to celebrate yourself in the presence of your good friends – you should celebrate more with them and express how great you feel about your worth.

In life you need friends, because you cannot stay alone. However, the friends you find should bring out the best in you. A good friend is the one that is looking for the opportunity to be the truest, the nearest, and the dearest to you. A good friend will have a lot of passion for you and will love you to bits. A good friend will never give up on you in tough times. A good friend will be one of the best things that has ever happened to you. A good friend will rekindle the fire that is on the inside of you and make sure that the fire does not die. He or she will keep inspiring you and help you to see yourself as the best. A friend will give you a reason to continue in life. Good friends are very hard to find, but I hope you will find one that will treasure you. I hope you will find someone that will always lift you up in life and will never throw you down. Words are a great source of healing, and that's the power that lies within a good friend. The words of a good friend are like a healing river that puts a stop to your tears. Even one friend is enough to make your life brighter.

I laugh, I love, I hope, I try, I need, I fear, and I cry. I know you do the same things, so we are not different. I understand the way you feel and also the fact that you might find it difficult to celebrate yourself. I know there might be issues in your life that are pulling you down. Maybe you have not arrived at the place you expected yourself to get to, and because of that you aren't happy. I know that it hurts and that you don't find things easy. Above all, I know you are stronger and more capable than you think. You are on the winning side.

You can only celebrate what you believe in. Believe in yourself so that you can celebrate yourself.

Chapter 2
Believe in Yourself

Believing in yourself has a lot to do with self-celebration. You have to believe in yourself. If you do not believe in yourself that much, this is the time for you to change that. You are worthwhile. Believing is a very strong thing. You have to believe that you are able in all aspects of your life. You have to believe that you are able to do what you do well. You must believe in your strengths and potentials, and in where you are going in life. You have to believe that you can do anything. Believing in yourself will give you energy to go for anything you wish for in life.

Believing in yourself will strengthen your courage. You will be able to face any situation when you believe in yourself, and you will not look back. You will say to yourself, 'I can do this.' You will be a strength to others. You can do it – you are more than capable. Try and go for that thing you really want, and you will see that everything will be fine.

Do not allow others to believe for you. I know you have good friends that you trust, and they can say to you, 'I believe in you.' That's fine, but you have to do it for yourself. You have to know who you are and be able to stand strong in the midst of others. You have to be able to represent your true nature and stand for where you are going in life.

You have to believe for yourself, in your personality, and in your uniqueness. This has a lot to do with accepting yourself for who you are. You are different, and it does not matter how negatively you or others may be thinking – believe in yourself.

You are different in a good way. Your personality is awesome, and you bring a different taste to the table. You are not like others – you are unique. Others do not have to like it. If you have not believed in yourself before, it is time you start. You can regain yourself. Believing in yourself has to do with agreeing with yourself. If you believe in yourself, you will not be against yourself. Even if others stand against you, you will still stand for yourself.

You simply have to love yourself to bits. Do not care what others think. You should not live your life based on what people say or do. Your life belongs to you and you have the right to live it as you want. If you believe in yourself, you will fight for yourself. If you believe in yourself, you will not have doubts about your achievement. You will say to yourself, 'That's what I've done, and I am proud of it; even my smallest work is of great virtue.'

Do not have doubts about your achievements. You have to believe in your achievements even when others are speaking negatively about it. That's their own business – do not care about what they think. It is up to you to think of your own world. Keep on celebrating. You have to believe that you are the best. In the midst of people, believe that you are there to give your best. No matter how much others judge or ridicule, you should not accept it. Keep your mind fixed on the good things about yourself, and know you are the best of your kind. Celebrate that.

You have to believe that it is possible for you to achieve your dreams. You have to believe that there is still a lot of time ahead of you to restore the things you have lost in life. It's not over, and you are not destroyed. With the help of this book you are about to re-start your life. You have to believe that you can cross over any difficulty you are going through at the moment. You have to believe that even if others do not stand by you, you can still make it. It is not every time that people are going to agree with you; it is normal for them to do weird things and sometimes hurt you. You must understand and keep going. Do not fix your mind on them; fix your mind on your own project and where you are going in life. Then, celebrate yourself.

You have to believe that there is a lot ahead of you. You are great and carry great potentials. There is a lot that you know, and people are waiting for your presence because they want to learn from you and get to know you. You have a lot to offer the world, so celebrate the fact that you are about to meet special people.

You might have the smallest talent in the world, but you still have to believe in yourself. Your joy is to see it as a big thing. You have to see your talent as a big thing. You might have achieved just a little in life, but still believe in yourself.

Your old has passed away, and all things are new. Nothing should stop you from believing in yourself. You have to believe in yourself every day and everywhere. You have to believe that you are a big person that the world is looking forward to meeting.

Do you believe in yourself? How far do you believe in yourself? I want you to start believing in yourself now. You can believe in yourself even more as you start to understand the purpose of believing. You should be proud of yourself. You are not just an ordinary person; you are on this earth for a purpose.

You should not look down on yourself for any reason; it does not matter whether something is your fault. I know you have made mistakes, but they should only encourage you that there is something greater in your future. You are able to reach excellence. You are able to reach for things that are better than your dreams. As you work towards excellence and produce the best results, believe in yourself throughout the journey, even when you make mistakes. Believing in yourself is a continual process.

Sometimes you can make others believe in you by taking the right action. You simply have to ask yourself, 'What am I doing wrong? What am I doing that is not up to my standards?' Then check the standard and make changes.

You have the power to believe in yourself. The power lies inside of you! I believe in you that you will show the world that you are of a great value. You will show the world that you believe in yourself. You are able to make it and also shine out to become the possible best.

Some people have passed the level that you are in life today, and you can learn from them. What did you see them do that made people believe in them? Learn from it and do the same. Copy the good examples, and also remember that those people made mistakes. You will not make those mistakes because you will be better.

You might have to push higher in order for people to believe in you. Maybe you are experiencing difficulty at your workplace, and your boss doesn't seem to believe in you. Make the necessary changes, and you will see that your boss will start believing in you. You will turn out to be the best.

You have to understand that there are wicked people in the world, and they might dislike your destiny or not want to believe in you. You don't have to worry yourself about them. Keep your focus and do not lose your mark. They might feel you are too great, and they might be scared of your destiny. You do not have to focus on such people – ignore them. Some people are ready to stand against your dreams, but don't worry about them and leave them alone.

You can turn your life around by copying the examples of successful people, and you will see that people will start believing in you. Do not take anything for granted. The smallest effort you make will bring the best to your life, and it will change your story.

Even your appearance can tell whether people will believe in you. Make sure your appearance is always excellent. Treat yourself in a special way, and you will see that people will start believing in you. Anytime you are going out, make sure you dress in your best. Make sure your face and your body look good.

If you feel you have done so much but people do not believe in you, then relax. You have to relax when you know that you have tried. Every trial is not a waste. Remember that when the right time comes, they will start believing in you. You do not have to stress yourself out. Be happy. Sometimes if people do not believe in you, you might need to try something else. You do not have to stay on the same thing all the time; you can try to make a change or introduce something new. The new thing you work on might sort out the problem.

You can even use your own words to make people believe in you. By speaking confidently, you will see that you will win the heart of others. Those that have not believed in you before will start believing in you; they will tell people good things about you. The power lies in your mouth and how you communicate.

I believe in positive stubbornness, which is when you do not allow the negativity of others to bring you down. In that sense, you are being stubborn in a good way. When you face enmity and when things do not work out easily, you need positive stubbornness. It will help you to believe in yourself. If you do not believe that others will believe in you, then they never will. In life there are various levels. Some people might not believe you today because you are not strong enough, but if you endure and allow yourself to grow stronger with time, you will see that the person will definitely believe in you. It will surprise you.

There is a popular saying that first impressions last the longest. The first time you do something is very important, and you should try your best so that the first impression of you will be excellent. This impression will enable people to spread your name because you have made them believe in your ability.

If you do not trust others, you cannot give them the opportunity to believe in you. You have to trust them no matter what. You still have to try to trust them regardless of your past. You have to try to move towards others so that whatever you want to achieve through them can be possible. I am not saying you should trust those that have abused you or used you wrongly. I basically mean trust the good people that serve as a source of blessing to you.

You can perform miracles. If you say to yourself, 'I will try to do my best, and I will be excellent in my action,' then a miracle will happen. Your miracle will surprise others, and they will start believing in you. I believe you can be powerful by overcoming your challenges and fixing your problems. I do not mean that you have to perfectly fix up all your problems, but you must make a little effort. When you come out powerfully, people will believe in you. Even when you feel completely crushed, you should still believe in yourself and not let yourself down.

Understand that your future is bright;
this will give you an unshakeable
confidence to celebrate yourself.

Chapter 3
Know That Your Future Is Bright

You can start celebrating yourself now, because your future is bright – there is no doubt about it, and nothing can change it. You deserve a great future because you are working hard at this moment and are doing your best. I congratulate you for every effort you are making! It is not going to be a waste. Your efforts represent your best. Never give up, and be full of encouragement. Things will work out right, and you are not going to be disappointed forever. You will experience great things that you have never before experienced.

Your hard work today is not going to be a waste. In the future, you will clearly see why you have been working hard. In the future, you will have a reason to say, 'I was only preparing then. now I understand why I went through that difficulty. Things look very clear now, and I am very glad of my life.'

You deserve a 'well done' for all those bad experiences you have been through. You deserve to see things work out better and to experience a brighter side of yourself. You deserve to see the best of yourself. Watch out – your life is going to glow, and you will shine against all odds.

Your lost wont compare to your gain. Your destiny has been preordained. Your days of hurting are no more. You will be restored. You will become respected and well known. You will achieve the impossible. The best will come out of you. You will not regret the past anymore.

I see you climbing high in life. I see you achieving your dreams. i see you becoming the better you. I see you getting your dream job. I see you receiving financial blessings. I see you achieving more than ever. I see your desires becoming true.

The impossible shall become possible in your future. Doors that have been locked for years are going to open. Opportunities that have been wasted will be regained. Things will be put back right again. You will look at your greatness and smile. Everybody will celebrate you, and you will be glad. Your challenges will be no more, and your heart desires will become a reality. You will see your dreams come true, and you will feel better on the inside. The efforts you have made in the past will lead to your success. You will no longer say 'I regret this' or 'I should have done this that way'. You will be satisfied.

You may be going through a lot of disappointments today, but I can tell you that there is a big yes in your future. Those that disappointed you in the past are going to come and check for you; they will call your name again and will celebrate you. They will have a reason to connect with you. Your future is going to work out, and things are going to be different.

You are going to celebrate yourself, and your future is very bright because the little efforts you are making now are not going to waste. You are not wasting time at the moment; every effort you make is a big thing, and it will add up to your future.

In your future, people will notice you and celebrate you. You have not suffered for nothing. The sufferings you have experienced in the past are going to make you into a brighter person. Your future is filled with a lot of great self-celebration. Your future will erase your past and cause you to shine brighter and greater. Your suffering is for a purpose. Someone that is in the dark cannot be bright. If you are in the dark today, you will not remain there forever. Very soon you are coming out, and you will be stepping into your future.

Your bright future will surprise many and cause them to ask for you. The brightness of your future will cause a shake in the world, and many will gather together because of it. Your future is going to be amazing and will describe you to the world in a greater way.

You can and will be different from what you are today. The old things that you experience today will pass away in your future. You will experience new things, and you will be very happy to celebrate yourself. Your future will say over to your past because it will bring fresh and beautiful things to you. I am filled with great joy to announce that you have a bright future. Your future will cause every part of your life to be bright; so keep preparing for the future.

So why not start celebrating yourself now, because you have peace of mind that your future will be bright. There is nothing to worry about. Cast your fears away and walk with your head held high. Be bold and strong because something good is awaiting you in your future; the dark clouds are going to clear off, and your smile will be big.

Every individual in life has a future. Even plants and animals have a future. You cannot be denied of your future, so do not allow anyone to put fear in you. Don't allow others to tell you that you don't have a future. Clean away the paintings people create, saying that you will never come out of your current situation and step into the future. People can take items away from you, but they cannot take your future away. Today you might not be a star, but in your future you will be one. Today you might not feel like a winner, but in your future you will be a champion. Impossibilities shall become possible in your future, and everything will be okay. No one will be able to destroy your star. Your future will be so bright that people will be afraid. They will be shocked about what will happen. Your future will enable you to leave great footprints of who you are; it will describe you to people in a new and wonderful way. As a star, you have capabilities, qualities, gifts, and talents in which the world is interested. You are a star because there is something you know how to do, and you are very good at. You are also a star because the way you think and feel is a unique one. You are very unique, and there is no reason for you to compare yourself to others.

Your future will be superior to your past. It will be filled with good memories and uncountable blessings. Brightness brings beauty to things. Your future will bring internal and external beauty to you. The old things in your life will pass away. You might not be experiencing breakthroughs at the moment, but in the future you will experience them. You will have breakthroughs over the difficulties you are currently experiencing. You will have financial breakthrough, meaning more money in your bank account. You will have marital breakthrough, meaning you will be married and well settled. You will have mental breakthroughs, meaning you will have a lot of peace and soundness in your mind. You will have academic breakthroughs, meaning those challenging subjects you are studying will become easy.

The light in your future will enable you to see clearly and stand soundly. The future is not going to be the same as today – you have to hope. I know that you might be thinking small about yourself, and you may feel that you cannot make it. You will make it, moreover and your future will be amazing.

You can add a lot of fun into your life. You can have fun in your house and also outside. You do not have to be bored. Do something that is exciting, something of which you are proud. Do something that will relax you. In turn, the activity will bring you joy and make your day interesting. You are the only one that knows what brings you fun. Do not exit fun – enter into it and have a great day.

Try to take a little step in preparing for your future.

Remember that every step you take draws you closer to your destiny and brings quality to your future. Every step is not a waste. Sometimes you might need to leave your friends so that you can have time to prepare for your future.

You can start celebrating yourself today. You should look at every area of your life and be proud of yourself. Be proud of the things you have done, because your future is going to be filled with lots of excitement. Allow others to also be proud of you. You should celebrate yourself because you are a success and will always be one. I can assure you that you will make it and will become a success. Your success will surprise many. Maybe at the moment you feel like you are the odd one out in your family; no one is celebrating you while others are being celebrated. In the future, it will not be the same. They will have great reasons to celebrate you, and they will speak good things of you behind your back. In your family, you will be an example and a source of pride. You will be a solution and not a problem. Your family members will turn to you, and they will be happy about how you have overcome obstacles. Your family will rejoice with you and see you as an important person. They will treat you specially and value you highly.

Your future will be glorious. In the future, you will carry a glory which will make others praise you. You will be praised outside of your home and also inside. You will be lifted up and not be cast down. Your brightness will extend far, and it will be a blessing to others. You will definitely be victorious over your past, and those that have looked down on you will be the same ones that will celebrate you. Your future carries a light that will spell out your name in a great way. You will be honoured in the streets and everywhere.

Your future will polish your weaknesses and turn them into strengths, and then you will remember your weaknesses no more. In the future you will be a source of encouragement to weaker people. You will be able to teach them and remind them that their future is bright. You will arise to become the perfect you. You will arise to fulfil your purpose, and your talents will not be hidden. You will become your best and will celebrate your days. You will not look at your past anymore. You will say to yourself, 'I am a winner.'

Your future makes you a giant in front of your enemies. Your enemies will be down in the future, but you will be up. Your future brings you honour. People will honour you because you will have your own kingdom. You will reign, you will rule, and you will become more powerful. You will be treated like a royal and not just an ordinary person. I want you to remember that you are a good person, and every good person deserves to be bright in his or her future. The good that you have done to others and also to yourself will not be a waste; it will bring you reward. In your future, people will ask what the secret to your success is. They will be trying to understand. The people that will be around you will benefit a lot, to the extent that they will not want to leave you. You will be loved.

The correction you have received today will also benefit you in the future. When people correct you, do not be offended or hurt. You don't have to feel bad about it. I know it's not easy to receive correction, especially when it comes from people who don't know how to do so in a nice way. Receive the correction with joy and know that it will bring benefit in your future.

Have peace of mind about where you are today. You do not have to worry about things you have not yet achieved. Do not allow the disappointment you have suffered to make you lose hope. Get your hope high and enjoy your day, because your future is bright. There is a lot of abundance in your future.

Do not be guilty about your imperfect side. You don't have to feel bad; you simply have to know that imperfections are normal, and we can't do without them. However, you should know that as you grow day by day, you will sharpen your imperfect side, and it will become perfection one day.

Try to discipline yourself every day for success by practising those steps that will make your future bright. Practise your talents and gifts, and then do them again and again. Have joy in doing them and be very cheerful. Remember that there is something greater ahead of you: your future.

Try to listen carefully. Be sensitive towards how things are done, and do not remain in your own world. Open up to new ways of doing things, and learn something new every day. By doing so, you will see that you can perfect your gifts and talents, and therefore you will have a bright future. You will prosper. Do not allow anyone to deceive you into believing you are not going to prosper. Do not allow negative things that are going on in the world to disturb your mind. Do not look at those that haven't made it. Focus on those that have made it and believe you will make it too.

**Do things that give you joy, and your
joy will lead to self-celebration.**

Chapter 4
Connect with the Things That Give You Joy

You need to understand the difference it makes when you connect with things that give you joy and happiness. I want to expose you to the things that give you joy. There are things that you do every day, but most of them might not be bringing joy to your life. You might find them boring. Instead, highlight the things that give you joy. It varies with individuals. For your friend it might be singing, but for you it might be visiting people. Then create the time to do such things. I can assure you that your life will have meaning and will make a lot of sense when you start doing the things that give you joy.

What are the things that give you joy? They are your gifts and talents. What have your friends told you that you are good at? Have you ever been specially selected to do something? That might be your talent. People can see your talent, and even you may see it. You know yourself best, so you should be able to know the things that are your gifts and talents.

The things that give you joy are things that you feel rewarded for anytime you do them: you feel blessed, touched, and new afterwards. You feel very proud of yourself anytime you do it, and you feel as if the whole world is on your side. You see yourself as someone who is on top of the world.

The things that give you joy will make your life free of stress. You simply have to spot these joyous things. Start doing them now. The things that give you joy are things you find natural. Your life will be free from struggles because the things that give you joy are easy for you, whereas they might be difficult for others.

You will find your best in the things that give you joy. You will stop comparing yourself to others, find yourself, and be happy with your production. You will look at yourself and say, 'Is this me. I have come this far.' Make sure you focus on the things that give you joy: your talents.

You might say to yourself, 'I find it difficult to connect to the things that give me joy.' However, it is very easy. What are your talents and skills? What are you good at? Make use of what you are good at. There are people who flow in the conversation whenever you meet them; get closer to them, because they are the people that give you joy.

Stay with people with whom you enjoy being around – they are the people that amaze you and make you think positively about yourself. Their words fill you with joy and remind you about your bright future. They do not waste your time; instead, they add value to your life.

Maybe there is a place you like going to because it reminds you of good memories, brings you excitement, and refreshes your mind. Make time and visit the place. Do not let anyone waste your time by making you go to a place that doesn't give you good feelings. You want to be happy, and that is the point of life. Therefore, be in the right place.

The things that gives you joy are things that inspire you in life and make you feel rewarded. You find them easy to do. Do those things again and again, because they give you joy and lead to self-celebration. That is what I mean by pure joy. Maybe you find joy in speaking positive things into your life, or maybe it's calling a friend or meeting up with people. Do it again and again. Everyone's source of joy is different.

Pleasure is also a source of joy. Things that you count as a pleasure are the things that will increase your joy. Do not allow anyone to deny you pleasure. It is very important for you to add pleasure to your life. You don't want to spend the whole day feeling bored and down. You don't want to feel like the whole world is against you. You don't want to feel like it's over. So, start using your gifts and talents today. Get your joy up by doing something that makes you eager.

You have to be very intentional and direct towards connecting with the things that give you joy. Life can be very miserable for people, especially when they are going through difficult times, if they cannot connect with what gives them joy. You will find joy in using your skill or talent, and you'll start flowing with joy. You will be able to express yourself well and joyfully when you use your talent in the midst of people. Your talent is never a waste – it is a precious gift. Joy will not come unless you press the right buttons. Then, others will start rushing to you when they see that your life has joy.

Show people what you've got; let them see your gifts and talents. Help them to know and understand you better. Use your gifts and talent to be a blessing and benefit to their lives. Express yourself with pride and don't be shy. You know you've got that talent, so go for it and try something new today.

Sometimes you cannot avoid an event of sadness, but you can still arise with joy. I know you have been through a lot in your life. You have experienced things that you do not deserve. You have been hurt and put down. I know these things have happened, but it is time for you to put that aside. Arise now with joy.

If you like giving to people, what you give is really up to you. If you are a joyful giver, then give deliberately to release your joy. There are hidden abilities in you, and most of them will make you a centre of joy. Do anything that gives you joy.

I am sure that you like to have a sense of celebrating yourself amidst others. When you start using your abilities to create joy, that will benefit you. You will not believe that great things will start happening in your life once you start living it with joy. You will be surprised. Joy will make you more active and will positively affect other areas of your life. In the absence of joy, there can be sadness. Stop doing the things that don't give you joy, and start focusing on the ones that do. Always try to create time for joy, no matter how busy you are. I know your life will be a joyful one, because you are making the effort daily to connect with sources of joy.

I know you have a number of friends, but I advise you

to spend more time with the ones that give you joy. The friends that leave you cheered up and with better feelings are the ones with whom you should spend time. Try to connect with your joy every day and in every way. Joy makes you strong because it is a great source of strength. Joy builds a foundation that can never be broken. Keep your joy with passion. Joy makes you feel victorious, and at least you will know that you are getting somewhere in the midst of life challenges.

You should always say to yourself, 'Everyone can be sad today, but I am going to be joyful. I will intentionally keep my sense of joy.' Joy brings comfort to you, and no one can take it away from you. Nothing in life can steal your joy – it belongs to you.

You might have some abilities. Ability means being able to do, or having some know-how. Your ability does not have to be perfect, but you can still try. People who become perfect in their abilities had to take a first step and try. They weren't that good, but as they practised, they became perfect.

What makes you feel proud of yourself? Spot that thing and start doing it; it will enable you to live in the moment and have a more fulfilled life. Your life will make sense, and your joy will be great. You don't have to look back at the time you made a mistake and let that stop you from trying. Some people are working hard but for nothing. All they are concerned about is how they will make money, so they get locked up in jobs that they do not like. The job does not relate to their destinies. Your destiny is the most important thing. You simply have to focus on your gifts and talents, making sure your job relates to it; then the job has a future impact and will bring you joy.

Don't allow the imperfections of your children to steal your joy. Children are a gift, and we all have been in their position once. Your children will definitely grow to become wonderful children that will bring reward to you. Don't allow what is going on at the moment to steal your joy.

Maybe you know people that often say bad things. Their presence does not bring any reward or joy to you; they do not make you feel blessed and special. Simply avoid them. I know it's difficult to get rid of people especially close ones. However, you can reduce the amount of time you spend with them. You have to know that your life is for you, and you have the power to close the doors on intruders that are trying to steal your joy.

If you are in the midst of people and do not feel treated the same way as others, such a thing can steal your joy. You have to handle those circumstances with maturity and still remember your special self. Don't allow the characteristics of others to bring you down; you don't have to lose your hope and joy because of them. If you are a manager at work, and you expect your staff to behave or act in a specific way, but do not do so, then do not be disappointed. Do not feel like it will never work out. Be patient and try to talk to them in a nice way. Don't allow the situation to take your joy away. Do your best to keep your joy.

Maybe you are going through a tough situation at the moment. The situation does not look like any that you have ever been through before. You don't have to say to yourself 'I feel like giving up' or 'I am completely tired of this'. You will get through it, but you will come out stronger, so keep your joy.

Maybe you have tried to win the hearts of people, and you are trying to make friends, but it doesn't work out. Don't give up. You have a lot of chances to make friends. You are not the only one experiencing such difficulty right now. Therefore, do not look down or yourself or say, 'I can't do it again.' The next time you try, you will make lots of friends. Try to keep your joy.

Sometimes in life you have to learn to ignore things, especially the negative things. If you take things too seriously, it is like hitting yourself. You do not want to get to a stage whereby it feels like everything around you is frustrating you, so be calm. Even when someone says something bad to you, you can laugh; by laughing you shame them and say, 'You haven't hurt me.' Then, you are joyful.

I know you have been through a lot of things in your past. Maybe you still remember them, and they hurt as if they are happening now. I do understand, but I want you to find joy in your life and create space for it. I want you to live a life that is fully maximised and free from hindrances. Don't allow anything to hinder your joy. You have to get rid of those things that you do not like. If you don't like it, then remove it. Stay with people you like, go to places you like, treat yourself the way you like, and enjoy what you like. Your life belongs to you, and you have the power to fashion it in a way that will bring you joy and something to always look forward to.

Follow those steps that give you joy. Your joy is a very important thing, and you should never miss it; it keeps you in shape and gets your balance right. It keeps you with a positive feeling on the inside and helps you to continue in spite of other areas that might look difficult.

Wisdom also gives you joy. Add wisdom to every area of your life; be wise and learn from people who reach their goals. Don't repeat the same mistakes that you and others have made in the past; try to appreciate a better way of doing things.

Work hard by trying your best. It might be painful, but it will bring you reward. Know that every good thing you are doing will become a big thing one day, and do everything to the best of your effort. As you push to the next level, you will see that you will enjoy the fruits of your labour. You will have joy in your life!

Learn to stand your ground. You do not have to be a people pleaser. Don't please everybody, but hope that others will be pleased by what you do. You can't satisfy everyone in life, and trying to do so can steal your joy. You have to stand firm towards your own decisions and go for what you want. Choose the best for yourself.

Fear can stop you from taking the first action that will lead to your success and self-celebration, so deal with that fear.

Chapter 5
Don't Allow Fear to Get in the Way

You are very great, and a great person like you does not deserve fear in his or her life. You deserve to be filled with boldness and a strong spirit that will bring your dreams to fruition. You will get rid of that fear and arise to become the perfect and shining version of you. Remember that you are brilliant and very capable, so don't let fear get in the way.

Fear can make you lose the reasons for self-celebration. Fear is likely to leave you feeling that you are worth nothing; it can grip you and make you feel like others are more important than you. It can make you feel that others are superior over you, and that you do not deserve to celebrate yourself. You were born to do things that are unthinkable, unimaginable, and inconceivable, so celebrate yourself for that!

Fear can destroy your thoughts and leave you in negativity. You do not have to live in fear. You can be one of the boldest people on this earth. When you get it right, you will see that the way you view yourself will change, and your fears will be erased little by little. The magnitude of the blessings that will enter into your life will be unexplainable, so look forward to that and celebrate it.

Fear is not a good thing, and I hope that you will not have it in your life. Fear is very dreadful and can prevent you from moving forward. You have to get rid of fear, and I will help you. When you get rid of your fears, you will see that you can do things that you have never done before.

Fear will prevent you from facing your enemies and dealing with them. You have to confront some enemies and ask them to take their hands off your life. In the case of fear, you will keep procrastinating and leaving it until a further date, which can be very dangerous. I don't want anything bad to affect your life. You have to be bold now, and that is exactly what is going to bring a turn-around into your life.

Do you know you are a great person? Great people go through negative situations. I have seen people go through terrible situations and come out fine, with joy and laughter. The situation did not kill them; it brought out the best in them. Every time you go through a bad thing, you become a better person, so you don't have to fear.

Maybe someone in your home or workplace has been making you uncomfortable. You might need to face the person and speak your mind. Let the person know that you are not happy with the situation, and ask them not to tamper with you anymore. Facing them might actually solve the problem compared to keeping silent. Do not live in fear and always pursue a bold life.

Fear can prevent you from possessing what belongs to you. There is a lot for you to possess on the surface of this earth, and if you are fearful, you cannot reach these possessions; you will imagine yourself there, but you will not be able to achieve anything because of the fear. Lose the fear today. If you face the future with boldness, the things you will achieve will be unbelievable.

There are people whose presence is frustrating. You need boldness to tell them not to come back to you again. You must deal with them. Do not let them put fear in you. Do not allow someone to keep you in hiding or to destroy the good things that you have in your life. You have the right to protect what belongs to you. You have to reach a place of full boldness, whereby you can express yourself to people.

Fear can make you believe the lies of others. You have to admit to your true nature in life. You are different, and there is nothing wrong in that, If you have fear, you will not believe in yourself, and you will not be proud of what you have achieved. Fear is hiding on your inside. You have to occupy the places of fear in your mind with boldness.

I have seen great people be treated like slaves because they have fear. Not all people care about us, and they are not careful to treat us right. If you possess fear in the midst of such people, they will use you and mistreat you; they will not add any value to you. However, you will do things in this life that will blow the mind of people, so start celebrating yourself for that.

You do not have to live under the control of others. There are people that like to be in charge, and they do not want to give others a chance to live free lives. People like that are very dangerous, and you have to be careful of their presence. You are free to be yourself and live your life as you wish, with boldness. Choose what you want. Your thoughts do not define what you will become, because you will do things that are greater and beyond your thoughts.

Fear can make you lose direction and focus. If you fear people, you will not be able to achieve what you want in life, and you will easily be affected by what they say and do, living under their fear. Say to yourself, 'I am not going to live under people. I am going to rule in my own world and be the best I want to be.' It's your time to be free from fear and to get to a place of self-celebration.

You can live a bold and a happy life. You are special and a winner, and you are in this world to succeed. Arise and become your best. Maximise the resources around you and use them to bring the best out of you. Shine in your life and ensure that you have a good time. Don't fear. In this life, you are going to do things that will be incomprehensible to the human mind.

Boldness will help you to live and think like a champion daily. You will be free and creative. You will be able to set up goals each day. You will achieve them and will climb higher. You will see yourself well settled and very happy. Your dreams will begin to happen to you. You don't have to follow the custom of those that live under the fear of people. Instead, be free to live your life the way you want, shining just as you are.

People run away from a place where manipulation takes place. If you do not have fear of such a place where others are scared, you will be able to grow and make a difference. You won't be controlled and pushed; you will be stable and can make something happen in a difficult place. If you are bold, you will be able to make possibilities happen in an impossible place.

When you find yourself in situations that look bigger than you, do not to be afraid. You have to be strong and remain patient. You must know that there is something ahead of you. You have a goal and a purpose, but you are faced with something. See it as a little thing, and before you know it you will walk through the situation like a bold lion. Allow the spirit of boldness to be planted so that you can live an elevated life.

Do not allow what others do to make you fear. Humans are nothing. We are all going to die one day and turn into sand. What do you fear in a man? Rise up! Do not be afraid, and know that you also have the same power that others have. You can be bold like that man or woman you saw. You can do it. You are able, and your own ability is likely to be stronger than others'. You are called upon to do extremely brilliant things in life.

Some people are afraid to talk. Do not be afraid to speak your mind in the midst of people – say what you want to say. Feel free and flow. Realise that you are capable and respected in their midst. You are there to shine just as you are. You can start practising it, and soon you will become very bold. The detailed picture of your life will be wonderful when you walk in boldness.

You are in life to overcome obstacles; you are not here to be a loser. When a strange situation comes your way, you don't have to run away. You must face it and know that you have the power to win over it. There are so many things that you have faced in life, but here are you today. You did not die, so do not be afraid of the next thing. Those situations will bring a reward of achieving greater and wider dimensions in life.

Maybe you are thinking of trying a new thing, but fear is gripping you. When people are in new situations or environments, they tend to be scared. Maybe you are afraid of making a mistake. If you make a mistake, you are only on your way to becoming a winner. The key is to not give up. Stand up and go do the new things you want to do. What is stopping you? Go now! You do not deserve to carry the load of fear. Your life is tailored for big and incredible things.

The fear of your past can grip you. Maybe you have done something that you regret. You simply have to remember now that the past is over; today is a new day, and tomorrow is a better day. You don't have to sit in the past or start thinking that your past is going to hit you again. Today, you can smile and feel free like others. You have dealt with the past, so let it go and don't fear it. Something important and worth a great celebration is about to happen to you.

Do you feel fear when you are walking all about? What sort of fear is it? It's time to identify it. I know it's not easy to get rid of fear, but you can make it. You have to pretend to be bold until you are actually bold. You have to say to yourself, 'I am not going to be afraid of anything. I am still going to try to do what I want to do.' You are going to step into a greater level as you deal with your fear.

Even the people who seem fearless have fear on the inside. Despite that, they spend time in the midst of people. They know that they have fear, but they still find themselves amidst people daily, carrying out their jobs. You can, too. You are going to make it through this, my dear. You will reach an inconceivable level of success and satisfaction when you do not let the fear get in the way.

Let me give you a key for overcoming fear: making sure you always dress nice. Dress in an acceptable manner, and you will see that you would not have fear of talking to people or going where people are. You will be free, happy, and strong. You would not be shy to say what you want to people. You will see yourself as a highly valued person that's filled with success.

Another key for overcoming fear is despite knowing that you have the fear of being in the midst of people, still go into their midst. Just be natural about it, and even though your mind might remind you that you have fear, ignore it and take a bold step to do what you want. Love your life and add passion to everything you do. Embrace the fact that you are going somewhere in life and are ready for it. You are going to do awesome things on the surface of this earth, so start looking forward to them.

I know a young guy who was very afraid to talk to employers on the phone. He said, 'I do not know who I am talking to, so I am afraid that they might not like me.' That's a serious fear. This young man was unable to ask for a job on the phone, and he limited his chances of finding a job. Who knows – if he made the phone calls, he might actually have found a job. They might like him, but fear blocked his opportunity. You are wonderful beyond your fears, so get rid of that fear today.

If you are in a place where everyone is dressing nice but you are the odd one out, then you are likely to have fear. You should feel proud of yourself in whatever you wear. So you are better off getting yourself some nice clothing to put on for the next time you meet people. Go to the market or shops to find something that you look best in, whether it is cheap or expensive. You can always do better with your dressing style, so try to improve it. Make sure you are looking best from head to toe. It's not the price of the clothing that matters; it's about how you feel in it. You are gorgeous, so let your look shine.

Do not allow your weaknesses to make you fearful. If you are performing less at work, and it seems like every other person is ahead of you, then it can lead to fear. You can remain in the job, but try to look for another job that can give you the opportunity to perform better. When you are at your best, you can never be afraid or fearful. You are a very great individual, and fear has no power over you.

If you stay in environments where people are complaining about you, maybe they feel you aren't doing your best, and they aren't happy with you. This sort of environment can lead to fear. You are better off leaving and looking for a new place where there is no complaint. No matter how long people complain about you, life is all about you celebrating yourself. If you believe that you have done your best, there is nothing to be afraid about. You are filled with special blessings, and so fear has nothing to do with you.

Motivation is also very important. If fear is getting in your way, spend time with people who will motivate you and fill your mind with positive thoughts; this will drive you to go for what you want in life. Where there is fear, motivation can empower you to stand above it. You can motivate yourself and stand high above the fears that you feel inside. You are very talented and gracious, so don't let fear stop you.

The day you learn to see rejection and failure in a new light is the day you will get rid of your fear. If someone rejects you, that does not mean the end has come; you can always try again. Don't allow the rejections and failures to build fear inside of you. Always live a victorious life. Even the most successful people today have experienced rejections in the past. You are a winner over your rejections and failures. Therefore, go out and try going for what you want without fear. Celebrate your life greatly and grow stronger without letting fear stop you.

Sometimes you might need to analyse the fear. Ask yourself, 'Can it harm me?' If the answer is no, then there is no need to fear it, and then you will feel comfortable. You can take a step forward and do what you want to do. Whether you fear animals or people, simply ask yourself, 'Can it harm me?' You can gain the boldness to face the situation and climb higher in your life. You can shine broadly without letting fear stop you because you, too, can have a great name in this world.

In a situation where others are not afraid of doing something and you are the only one that is afraid, you don't have to be afraid. Try to take a step and join the queue. I am not bringing you down because of your fear; I am only trying to place boldness inside of you. I want you to be fearless and to feel free. I want you to be able to go for those things that you desire in life. I don't want you to live a life whereby you will be wishing for things but can't get them. You will go far in life, and you will achieve the impossible.

You can overcome your fears little by little – it will not happen in one day. It takes practise and time, but I can assure you that you will see a great difference in your life if you can try to take a step of boldness. You have to believe you can do it, and then you will be able to do so. You can achieve things that are beyond your mind. You can lead yourself to great heights in life. You can do the big things and enjoy the best things in life.

The things you fear are usually the best things: there are great opportunities, but you are afraid to tap into them. You feel that something bad might happen to you when you take a step, or you feel the people involved might not like you. That fear is not for you. Boldness is your portion, and with time you will overcome your fear. You will come out bold and win. You will overtake those that have gone ahead, and you will be a champion and a living testimony.

You have tried in life. Well done! Celebrate yourself for it. Trying is great.

Chapter 6
Remember That You Have Tried

You have to celebrate yourself because you have tried. You have come this far, and I say congratulations to you for that! I see that you have done great things, and you deserve a big 'Well done'. You have been through a lot, and you are still alive and making efforts every day. You have been able to deal with your difficulties. You have tried and done very well. You are very excellent and precious, so always celebrate yourself every time you have tried.

You have been tested in every way, and yet you have come out as a winner. Life is full of tests. Maybe you should have given up, but you did not – that means you have passed the test. Some situations could have got you down, but you did not allow it; instead, you rose to the challenge. You have tried. I congratulate you! You are taking those little steps, and you are trying to work things out. That's a great effort, and I know your future will be filled with wonders and extreme beauty because of this.

You have stood pure and did not mingle with bad things. You kept your path clean despite your difficulties. Not every step you took in life was easy, but you made great efforts. You have been genuine and did not change your words. You stood firm through everything. You have tried. I should carry you up high and ask the whole world to sing you a wonderful song, because you have tried in life.

You stood your ground even in the times of hard trials, and that tells me that you have tried. You have been trusted by your family and friends, and even though they expected you to quit, you did not. You have done a lot, you have done well, and you have tried. You will be the first in your future, and you will overcome your little challenges because you have tried in life.

You can never avoid trials in life. They do come, but that doesn't mean you should feel down and lose your excitement. You still have to keep yourself going despite the hard trials. You do not have to focus on the trials — you have to focus on your self-celebration. You have to always celebrate yourself and feel very up, because you are amazing. You deserve so much more and will achieve those things that you deserve. You will see something exciting in your future.

You are dependable. People have depended on you, and

they have been blessed in different ways through you. Your way of life is an example to other people and has taught them how to live their lives. You have been a living testimony, so well done. You will see that you will be above in life meaning standing out. You will achieve things that are beyond measures.

You have lived a perfect life, and many people look to you. You have come out stronger on the other side of your problems, and that is why you have to celebrate yourself. You are an interesting individual, so why not start celebrating yourself today? You have come a long way, and that should give you lots of joy and something cheerful to look forward to.

Other people can prove who you are because they have seen you in the different areas of your life. In life, you need witnesses. When people can testify about you and your deeds, you are a winner. To some extent we all need people, and we cannot do without people regarding day-to-day stuff. You are going far in life, and you will destroy your enemies through what your tomorrow holds.

Your trials have made you firm. You are unshakeable and are not easily moved by what people say, because you know who you are. You have come this far, and it's been a long journey. The more you go through, the stronger you become. You are sharper than you were before. You know how to deal with life and what it brings your way, so well done for all that you have done. You have done a very good work, and you will be seen and known for it.

Your strength is high because you have won over many battles. You have developed patience, and you know how to wait until things turn around for your good. You have survived, and you have made it — congratulations. Remember that these things you went through were not easy, but you have come this far. You will do greater things in your tomorrow, you will run your race, and you will receive medals for it.

You have survived on your own, and you have learnt lessons that have shaped your personality. Your personality has become better because you have changed your bad aspects into good, and you are even more understanding than before. You can deal with people properly and can talk well with them. You know how to handle things. Well done, and I look forward to you celebrating yourself in a bigger way in the future.

You've become someone whom people can depend on, and you are happier today because of the trials you have been through. You are more faithful because you have seen a reason to believe in yourself all the time. The reward of life comes to those who have been tried. Well done, and your own reward will even be greater than others'. You will be rewarded in a fine and adequate way.

I want you to know today that you will receive a reward for every trial you go through in life. If you feel you have not been rewarded, then your reward is on the way. You can never miss it. The reward includes good things that will come to you due to the seed you have sown during your hard trial. Your labour is not going to be in vain; your efforts are appreciated. You will be celebrated by millions, and they will call your name specially.

You are going to receive a change or a miracle due to your efforts. Remember that every little drop of water makes a river. For every step that you have taken, you will receive success and victory. Therefore, start celebrating yourself today and remember that there is a lot attached to your future. There are finer and greater blessings waiting for you.

The trials of life build your endurance and make you wait until you get what you want. Do you wonder why some people wander in life? It is because they have no endurance. You have been able to endure even when it looked like nothing good was going to come out. You have achieved something, and there is even more in your tomorrow. You will be lifted and honoured everywhere you go, and you will be approached in a fine way.

Problems can start in places you do not expect in life, but if you happen to be an individual that has no endurance, you will give up. If you want a beautiful future, then you have to endure. Maybe you are going through a sickness at the moment. I want you to endure and still keep your happiness. Keep singing your songs of happiness and celebration. Put a smile on your face. Remember, you will experience abundant greatness and celebration in your tomorrow.

I remind you that after your endurance has been tested, you will come out of that sickness or out of that problem. You will be free because it will soon be over. Despite your disappointments, you can prove that you are genuine. Your faith in your dreams will be genuine after people have tried everything to make you give up, but you still come back. You have to follow up with things until they happen for you. Never cut down your expectations because of what you have been through. Keep the best and greatest expectations for your life.

You return with a smile on your face, and you stay happy. You might feel as if you are in a prison today, because your dreams are not coming true. I want you to know that you are going to come out of that prison. You will not remain there forever; it cannot last forever. You are not going to remain in an odd situation forever; it is not possible. You carry great potentials and abilities on the inside, and someone like you deserves to be known and celebrated in life.

A true dream owner is someone that has passed through the fire and yet still comes out confessing his dreams to be genuine and unchanging. People have watched you make efforts in life, and they remember this. They know your dreams and are aware that you are a dreamer. They know you have a place to which you are going. You have really tried, and you have done very well in several aspects of your life. Therefore, celebrate yourself greatly today because of what is on the inside of you.

Your positive thoughts towards your dream still remain the same despite your failures. You still hold that precious thought towards your dream and destiny; you have not changed them despite your trials. You are still who you are, and you still think of yourself as that great dreamer that wants something specific in life. You have not given up. You have tried because of that, and in your future you will be one of the happiest people on the surface of this earth.

You have tried despite all the negative things. Sometimes

the mind can be very deceptive, and your mind told you that your project would not come through, and yet you made it come true. You are not on the same level you were before – you have moved ahead. You have searched yourself, and you have identified the areas of your mistakes and made improvements. Well done for those things that you have done. You are going to run with overflowing joy that will be unstoppable in your future.

You have tried to make changes even without others telling you; this means you have tried, and you deserve to be celebrated by yourself and others. What a great reason to celebrate in life. You are not a down person, and your position is up. You are a winner, and I tell you there are a lot of medals waiting for you in your future. You will be celebrated more and more. You will go beyond the normal level of success, and your life will be brighter. The quality of your life has come out as a result of the trials you have been through. Do you know that trials bring quality? Each time you are tried, you become better, and you are worth self-celebration. You become one of the best and outshine the crowd. You and the great seeds inside of you are worth a great deal. You are priceless and deserve the best. You are worthy and marvellous.

Even your leaders go through trials. The fact that someone

is leading does not mean she does not go through trials. People go through trials just as you do. You might find a trial painful, but that pain will turn to a glory for you. You will be a great glory, and your name will never be erased on the surface of this earth. You will be remembered forever.

The spirit of achievement that lies inside of you cannot be destroyed despite your trials. Instead, the spirit of achievement improves and becomes a strong tree that cannot be broken. I know that you have things on your mind that you want to achieve. You have interests and can come up with a picture of what you want your life to look like. You will be fantastic in your future, and you will reach for things that are unbelievable.

Since you have tried in the past, you don't have to remember the past anymore – you have to look at what is ahead. Even the smallest attempt you have made is appreciated. I appreciate people that have made the smallest effort; they are people who have succeeded because they tried. You should always see the small things you do as a big thing. You do not have to stress yourself in order to succeed in life; the little things you do can build up a fortune for you. Your future will be huge because you have tried.

Go for that job interview, because the company might hire you. You cannot compare people who have tried with those who have done nothing. Once you try, you have to know that you've done something great. You can even choose to do nothing, but your effort is worth celebrating. Do those things that you wish to do. Visit those places you wish to see. The moment you try, you have won and have come a long way. You will experience brilliant things in your future for it.

Life has a lot of opportunities, and all you have to do is try. Do new things every day. You can easily get bored if you are doing the same things over and over again. Make new friends often; the new ones you make might make a difference. You are not going to miss opportunities that come your way. You will step into those opportunities and give them your best. Then you will climb higher and use it to make your life prosperous.

Speak positive things into your life every day. As you do so, you will be better able to deal with challenges. I know life is not easy, and I understand how you are feeling. You do not have to be perfect the first time you try; you simply have to make an attempt. Your effort will lead to success in your future. You deserve a round of applause anytime you try. I appreciate you for that – keep doing the wonderful work you are doing.

Every effort you make to prepare will bring greatness to

your future. Every effort you make to change a bad habit will lead to eliminating that habit. Every effort you make to arise with your talent will lead to your recognition. You will not be hidden; you deserve to be famous and recognised all over the world because of the gifts and talents that you have. You will be fabulous in your today and also in your future.

Every effort you make to educate yourself will lead to a significant and impressive future. You are not a failure; the fact that you failed on your first effort does not mean you will fail again. You are not a castaway; your effort is a great thing and has shocked others that chose not to do anything at all. Your effort has given you a name above all names, and it will bring something fabulous to your future.

Your effort has erased your mistakes and given you a fresh start. Your effort made others understand you and see your interest in your project. The next effort you make will open a great door before you. Your determination to use your talents and abilities is very special. You are a very special individual – you have to believe it. Your life is surrounded with the stones of greatness; all you need to do is build your life using those stones. You are very precious.

Your result from your effort is a tangible sign of where you are going in life. Your consciousness towards your career today will lead to a powerful entry in your future. You will not fail and will surely become a success. You will see yourself shine against all odds. You will overcome and will come out as a winner. You will be a superstar, climbing against those walls that hold you back. You will come out as someone precious and more worthy than a diamond.

You have been serious about your career or dreams, and that will bring good results and high productivity your way. Your seriousness is not going to be a waste of time; it will bring a high level of productivity into your future, making you more prosperous than ever. Mentally, you are ready to give your best, which is a very good thing. Your effort to keep pressing forward will be rewarded. You will surely be a star and will be honoured. As you press forward, you will overcome your challenges. You will not be small – you will stand out tall. Your effort to be positive towards yourself, to develop better relationships, to form better habits, to embrace the place where you are, to develop your inner life, and to stay passionate about life will bring an increase into your life. You will see a clear change and will become better. You will excel and wax strong in the different areas of your life.

Some people might call you a lazy person because of your little efforts; do not mind them. Little efforts do not make you lazy – they only make you a genius in the process because they take you through the process and make you a strong candidate. Your effort develops the greatness on the inside of you and makes you a champion. I want you to embrace yourself warmly and be very proud of who you are.

Maybe you are saying to yourself, 'I've tried and failed.' The next time you try, you will not fail. Don't allow failure to stop you – you can try again! Feel free and feel great. Stop reminding yourself of your failure, and don't tolerate people that keep reminding you of your failure. You are not a failure. Failure is success in disguise. You are as precious as the most beautiful flowers, and your life is about to start. You have to believe that you will celebrate even more when you fail, because that means there will be lots of winning in your future.

It's not easy to make efforts in life, and I understand that you have managed to make certain efforts. You have been consistent, and that's a good thing. You have acted intelligently and have made a difference in your life, following through with your dream. You have been persistent and hardworking ever since. That's something precious for you to celebrate. You have done very well, and there will be lots of victories in your future. You will experience new breakthroughs and will stand high.

Maybe you do not feel like you have done enough. Maybe you feel you have not tried enough. I want you to feel good about the things that you have done. Try to build a sense of satisfaction. Feel satisfied about the fact that you brushed your teeth in the morning; that's a job on its own, and you have done well for that. You simply have to be happy with yourself and should not allow the judgement of others to bring you down. Nobody has the power to bring you down because they do not own you. You own yourself and are responsible to yourself. You have done very well with your life, so congratulations for that.

When you meet with your friends, talk about your achievements. Do not feel like you are the odd one out; let them know that you have done well and you feel good about it. Be proud of yourself all the time, feeling as if you are the best. Feel on top, and feel as if you have tamed a lion. Feel like you have overcome many challenges in life. Feel strong and very happy, and keep your emotions high. That's how to celebrate yourself in life.

I want you to know that you are a high person. You are not low; you are on top. You are not down. You are excelling, not failing. You are shining, not dull. You are full, not empty. You are able. You are the very best of your kind. You are unique amidst millions, and it is very difficult to find someone like you. The way you think and feel makes you a unique and blessed individual. You are too special to look down on yourself. You will be very great.

It's too late for you to say you have not tried. You have done very well, and you deserve to be informed that you have tried. From childhood you have followed a good path, and your dreams are going to come true. You will make it! You will be known in a unique way, and you will climb higher and reach for the impossible. You will be filled with beautiful colours, and your life will be beautiful like a rainbow.

Always hope more in life, and your hope will give you something to look forward to. That's self-celebration.

Chapter 7
Hope for More

If you feel like things are over for you today, then I want you to have hope. It is very possible for you to make it again – it's not over yet! You have to muster up some hope and start moving again. Don't let the situations you are going through kill your hope. There is no mountain that you cannot climb. You are capable, you are strong, and you are brilliant.

You should expect something greater for tomorrow. Everything will work out, and something new will pop out for you. You should hope that something beautiful, a miracle, will come your way. Always expect changes, and those changes will come due to your expectations. Keep working hard, and one day you will see the fruits of your labours come true. You are not going to regret; you are going to come out as a winner.

The people that have given up on you in the past will still

return back to you. They will love you again and will speak better things about you. If you make an effort, you will see that it will turn out in your favour. Something good will happen. Those that have given up on you in the past, feeling that you couldn't amount to anything, will come back looking for you. They will still celebrate you and will know that you are very precious and special.

In a situation whereby you feel everything is over, you simply have to rise and start again. Do not think that other people do not go through situations where they feel like giving up. It happens that way to all of us – we all go through it. The point where you feel like it's over is when new things are about to happen in your life. There will be a difference in your life, and you will see a change. You will fly in life and shine greatly.

Even when you behave your worst, you can still hope that you will do better next time. Bless yourself and praise yourself for the effort you have made. Recognise the fact that you made an attempt, and love yourself more. We all do not have the best behaviour, because sometimes we make mistakes. Even people that we look unto and assume are the very best do things that they shouldn't; they make mistakes, too. Don't feel like it's over because you have made a mistake. Believe in yourself, and you will get to your destination.

Maybe you took an action that you should not have taken. Maybe something happened, and you made a rush decision. You did not think about it and made a mistake. Probably the action is wrong and doesn't fit the situation; making things worse. You do not have to look back and regret what you have done. You should say to yourself, 'Oh, I blew it. But next time it will be better. I know I am on the right side.' The greatness in you will never stop – you are about to reach the maximum.

If you do not have the capability to do something specific, and it seems like others are doing it better than you, then you do not have to look down on yourself. You can make a decision to either stop doing it or look for something else to do that you can do better. You still have to hope in yourself. You still have to believe that you have your good sides. You have great talents and gifts that you can use to operate in a different area. You have something precious in your hand, and you should always believe that you are the very best, even when you are in the midst of the crowd.

Do not allow your incapacities to make you feel that you are useless. You are more than that, and you are very precious. You are more special than you think! Your incapacities have nothing to do with your life; they only show your strength in disguise. Do not allow your incapacities to make you feel like you are powerless. Your incapacities don't mean that you are a failure. You are on top, and forever you will be on top. You aren't going down; you aren't going to be destroyed. You are just about to make it, and you will experience success all the way.

You can be poor and still be hopeful. Maybe you do not have enough money in your bank account. You see others having more and buying more for themselves. Maybe your friend looks down on you because of that. You don't have to be disappointed or feel like it's over. You still have to believe in yourself and see the positive side. I know that you will have lots of money in your future, and you will even be able to bless others with money.

You do not have to judge yourself according to what your friends say. You simply have to say to yourself, 'I am going to make plans to get richer, and even if I do not have much today, there is overflowing abundance in my future. There is lot more in my future. My future is rich. My future is substantial.' Your future will be greater beyond your imagination, and you will get things about which you have not even thought. You will achieve the impossible and will overcome.

Hope is all about seeing something good in a place of nothing. Even in the darkest place, where you see that there is no light shining on you, you can still have hope. You simply have to keep hope for yourself. You have to see a possibility in a place of impossibility. You have to see a candle in a place filled with darkness. You have to expect that something will happen. Something good will happen to you. Your expectations or dreams concerning the situation will become true as you believe. They will not fail you. You will rise to become what you hope for, and you will see that your tomorrow will work out for you and will bring favour your way.

Never ever let a day pass you by without you having hope. You simply have to hope more. A life without hope is likely to be miserable. You should be happy and joyful so that your mind can be healthy and sound. Therefore, you have to put your hope in action by saying and doing positive things in order to erase the bad situation you are experiencing. You have to get yourself up. You have to look up in the sky and see a life that is adorable and happening for you. You will make it through your ordeals.

Remember that nothing is permanent. No matter how bad your situation is, it is not permanent and will not last forever. The problem is not going to keep kicking you forever. One day it is going to stop, and it will be over. Your fresh and happy life will start, and things will start turning out your way. You will laugh, be excited, and be joyful. You will arise to become all that you want to be, and you will be a place of joy and honour for many nations.

The situation will not repeat itself. That is part of you hoping more, and you have to activate your hope and know strongly inside of yourself that your situation is only temporary. Its only there to test you, and you are going to pass the test. You will fly out in many colours; you will outshine the crowd. You will become greater and will overcome your challenges. You will be very victorious. You will see the other side of greatness and will enjoy your life to the full.

You are a very good person. Although you cannot always determine what life will bring – because it does bring some difficulties – you should still know that the good that you possess on the inside will draw some goodness to you one day. A good person like you should always hope for something wonderful in life. You should believe that the best of the best will reach your hands very soon. You will walk in greatness and will be celebrated all over the world.

Bad things do happen to good people, but one day the bad will leave, and then the good rewards will follow. The bad will not keep hunting you. It will leave you, and you will regain your peace and stand up again. You will know that you are someone of great value. The bad things that are happening to you at the moment are only preparing you for one of the most beautiful experiences that this life will give to you. It is only preparing the king or queen on the inside of you.

With hope, you will face the world; you will be firm and courageous. You will stand your ground and will not allow anything to push you to the ground. Your troubles will fade away from your memory like the floods that have passed and will be remembered no more. You will look up and shine. You will be brave and full of might. You will discover the greatness on the inside of you. You will see that you are too precious to give up or to let go. You will enter into your own palace, and you will become a chief. Your life will be brighter than sunshine, and life's darkest hours will shine like the dawn. With hope, the darkest place will still bring light to you. You will experience something bright in life. You will arise and will be one of the best. You will see yourself on the other side, and you will be filled with good songs. You will create what you want for your life. I know you love the sun when it's shining, but your own life will shine brighter than that. The testimonies you will have in your life will be very vivid in the eyes of people. It will be very intense and will touch the hearts of many. Your life will be an example, and your bad past is going to be over.

Some people do not have hope because they lack security; they feel insecure and have issues in their life that are pulling them down. Do not allow your inconveniences to make you feel insecure. We do not have everything going well in our lives all the time. We all have at least one or two issues. I don't know your insecurities, but I know that there is nothing for you to feel insecure about. Don't feel shy, because you are not in the place where every other person is. In your time you will get there. You will even go beyond the normal experience of success.

I want you to feel secure and strong every day of your life. Feel secure every second. Do not be afraid of anything, and do not allow situations to take away your hope. Your hope is for you, and no insecurity has the power of taking it away. I want you to know that you are going to excel and will overcome so many of the challenges you are experiencing today. You will have a good life history because your end is going to be better than your beginning.

You do not have to despair, thinking that there is no way out in your situation. Don't keep those bad ideas in your mind telling you that you will never get anywhere. Do not tell people negative things about yourself, talking about how you feel so down. Instead, speak of hope and keep their minds hopeful. Keep something positive for yourself, and keep a positive story about yourself to tell others. You are extraordinary.

There are a lot of good things inside of you – more than you can imagine. You can fix your situation and awake with boldness. You simply have to try. You have to hope that soon you are coming out of your current situation. You have to believe that there is a possibility. You have to hope that new opportunities will come your way. You have to hope that new doors will open for you. You have to hope that the good gifts and talents that are on the inside of you will come out one day. You are exceptional.

I want you to look at the areas of your life that look dead, and I want you to say to yourself, 'It is going to live and grow again.' Nothing is over as long as you are alive. Even the worst situations have hope. There is always hope for you. You have to show your hope in the midst of others and let them know that you have hope. If they ever speak badly of your situation, tell them, 'I still believe in myself, and I know that my situation will live again.' It can only get better because you know that you are a powerful being who is able to bring a change into your own life. Let people see your hope. Let them know you as someone that always has hope. Give them something exciting to look forward to when meeting you. Let your hope shine today, because you are great.

If you are saying to yourself, 'Where is there any hope for me? Who sees any?' Other people know there are great things in you and that you are full of capability. They know you will make it through the hard times. Your enemies know that you are a winner and will make it through. There is hope for you! You should be optimistic about your today and tomorrow. You should always desire that something great will happen to you.

Some of the people you know have experienced bad things before, and they have come out of such situations. There is a lot of hope for you. You are very important in this world, and nothing can stop your hope. You have to hope and wish to come out of your situation. You will come out of it and will end up becoming a great person. You will be greater than you were in your past. You will achieve higher things, and you will tame lions. You will be the winner.

Some situations you are going through might try to uproot your hope. It may leave you thinking that it is over; it can leave you dry and make your face look like one with no peace and joy in life. That's not for you. You can still hope again, against all odds. Arise and begin to speak positive things into your life. Get up from the dark and rise into the light. See that there are lots of good things on the inside of you, and you have what it takes to challenge any bad thing that comes your way.

Maybe you built a lot of things in your life, and suddenly everything crashed down. You will still get those things back. I want you to know that there is hope for you. You still have a chance to get it right again, to rebuild those things. You are not going to lose anything; your life is not broken down. Nothing can smash your life down. The things you will have in your tomorrow will be greater than what you had in your past. You will make it. Everything that you have lost will return back to you through the efforts you make, and you will surely arise to be one of the best. You will regain what you have lost, and you will even have more stuff. Those that have witnessed you lose will witness you gain again.

If you have a fear that you are going to die due to some sicknesses, I want you to know that you are not going to die. There is a lot ahead of you in your life, including lots of good things. There are things that you have not yet discovered about yourself. You are about to see the best of yourself come out, because you are excellent and special. Your sickness is only a test of your character. It will disappear when the right time comes.

Maybe you are studying at the moment, and you do not have hope that you will get a good job when you finish your studies. It will not be that way. Maybe, people that you know never had good jobs, but your story is going to be different. You are going to succeed and will get the best. You have to say to yourself, 'I know that when it gets to my turn it's going to work out for me. My story is not going to be like others. I am hoping that the best job will come out and welcome me. The bad things that others have experienced are not going to be the same for me.' Always hope higher and believe strongly that you will receive the most beautiful things.

Do not allow yourself to be sad or troubled. Sadness can occur as a result of bitterness or unhappy feelings. Your mind can also be troubled when it seems the situation is going to leave you on top of the roof with a bad name. some situations can expose your weaknesses in life and even tend to bring disgrace to you. You must believe in yourself and hope that something beautiful will happen to you. You have to keep looking forward and loving yourself.

You can sing a song as a sign of hope. There are lots of songs out there that are filled with hope. The songs make you feel better on the inside. You should focus on such songs and play them at least once a day. These songs will remind you of the good things about yourself. The songs set you up on a positive road and make you feel great. You are very clever, so get some hope. Your life of hope will be an example to so many. People like others who are hopeful. They always want to be around people that are ready to speak very positive things into their bad situations. They do not give up, keep going, and see the things that they have spoken come to pass. It will come to pass in your own life as well. You will have a great and blessed life.

A lack of hope can lead to a feeling of rejection, making you feel as if everyone has given up on you. It will make you look like you are the only one going through. You have tried your best, yet you aren't getting results. I want you to know that your feeling of rejection is not something you deserve. Do not lack hope in your life – always press the button of hope, and your life will be amazing.

You are not alone, and I want you to keep the company of others and act like a winner. You are not an outsider or the odd one out. You are the blessed one. You are not rejected because you are the best and someone special. You are an individual filled with greatness. You are important and not just ordinary.

In a time of no hope, always remember your former victories, because they will motivate you to carry on and help you speak positive things into your life. They will light you up and give you refreshment. You must know that if you can win in the past, you are here to win again, and you will overcome your current situation. The fact that you were triumphant in the past means that you will be triumphant again. You will still defeat those situations again, and you will be a strong winner.

Maybe you expected your boss at work to promote you, but he did not. You just have to keep doing the job and know that one day he will promote you. If you are a good person, you can never miss a good thing. It might look like it is coming late, but something good is still going to happen to you. The promotion might come in another way or through another individual, but you will still get it. You are doing the best. Yours might come late, but the lateness does not mean you will be denied of it. Lateness is not denial at all; lateness does not mean it's over. Lateness prepares you to be able to keep things well and protect them. It makes you better than those who received it early. Lateness can make you the best and helps you to join the crowd of successful people. It leads you to great places. You will be celebrated in this life because you are believing in good things for yourself. You are very special.

Hope is a protection. Hope defends you in bad times and protects you from the wickedness of this world. When things don't look easy, if you have hope, you will keep smiling. Hope makes a way for you when there is no way. Hope says it is not over, even when others say that it is. You can still stand firm with hope.

Hope is a source of strength. When you have hope, you will be strong. No matter what comes your way, you will be able to say, 'Give me a break. I am a great person. I am going through this, but it is only temporary. Very soon I am coming out in beautiful colours.' You are very special, and a special person like you deserves to be lifted through life.

Hope makes you eager and gives you something to look forward to, no matter how dry you feel. Dry means not being productive. Maybe you feel small in your current situation because nothing is happening at the moment. Hold on to your hope, and with time you will see that something beautiful and great will come out of you. Something good will come your way, and you will be filled with wonders.

You will rejoice and be glad for many reasons, because you have held to your hope. You are going to be happy, and others will rejoice with you. You will experience something wonderful and will feel great about yourself and your life.

Sometimes when we go though situations, we feel as if no one is going to rescue us. I want you to know that you will be rescued from your current problems. You are not going to stay in the dark forever. As you hope, someone will come and help you one day. Someone will attend to your needs and get you off the hook. You will be moved to a greater level.

You must see yourself coming out of your situation. How do you do that? You have to hope that a change will happen. Some good people will come your way one day. Believe that someone is going to favour you one day. Know that it will work out for your good. People that are hopeful are usually happy people. They have nothing bad to think about; their minds are free, and they know that they will get some favour someday. They know, and their knowledge has made them strong. They believe in themselves and do not allow people to treat them poorly. Don't allow anyone to mistreat you, because you are fabulous. Hope takes pleasure in those that honour it. When the time comes, things will change, and you will not feel crushed for life. You will get better things in your hands, and you will enjoy the goodness of life. You will rule and win in the midst of others. You will always be triumphant.

When hope is crushed, the heart is crushed. You are likely

to feel helpless and alone when your hope is crushed. Do not allow big circumstances to crush your hope. Always protect your hope and keep being hopeful. You are always going to be hopeful because you are very special. Do not allow the words of people to make you lose your hope in terrible situations. What you are expecting will come to you one day. It's not a joke – it's going to happen! You simply have to remain positive and keep your high expectations. You are going to be great.

You might think no one is seeing your good deeds. You do not know it, but there is someone watching you and observing your ways. Your good work has been noticed and recognised by someone. One day, that person is going to speak for you, and you will be celebrated in this life in a special manner. In a time when you are going through tough things, keep hoping that someone will announce your name one day in a great way. You are going to come out of every situation you are experiencing. You will see yourself succeed, and you will become very triumphant. You are going to excel.

While you are hoping, you should also prepare well. Prepare yourself for a favour and to meet someone. You have to hope and at the same time make an effort to take an action so that when the hope balances with your action, it will bring a good result. Make sure your appearance is comely and decent enough. Always shine and look like someone that has risen. You will be celebrated wonderfully.

You should also hope that your talents will one day connect you to a greater person. Someone special will discover you and be happy to see you use your talents. Your talents are not just there for ordinary purposes; they're there to connect you with kings. They will align you with great people and bring you respect and fame. Hope gives birth to great things. If you hope for something, do not let others talk you out of that hope. As long as you want it, keep hoping for it until it happens. You are blessed.

Part 2

Why Should You Celebrate Yourself?

You are very special, because the way you think and see things are different from others, and that's the top reason why you should celebrate.

Chapter 8
You Are Very Special

You should celebrate yourself because you are very special. The day you realise you are very special is when things turns round for you. There are special abilities inside of you. You were not made for nothing. You were made to become something special in this world. You may not know it, but you are a star. That is why you cannot find anyone else that thinks the way you do. Your thinking is totally different. Your opinions are different, and you do not have to wait to become like others. You are perfect as you are.

It is very hard to find people like you. You have the ability to stretch to the next level and achieve higher things. Your next level is attached to your dreams and goals in life. The way you present yourself in the world is very unique, and that's the wonderful thing about you. You will get to places you cannot believe; I am speaking this into your life. You are very special, and because of that you will leave a mark on this world. You will make a difference, you will do great things, and you will be celebrated by many.

You can achieve whatever you want to achieve. There are things you feel you cannot do in life, and it will surprise you when you start doing them. Nothing is impossible as long as you believe it can happen. You are advised to remain focused and know that whatever you have said you will do in your heart will become a reality. You can make it just like anyone else. Others went through the same challenges you are going through at the moment. That is why you are not alone in what you are going through. There are things you feel you cannot achieve which you *can* achieve. You can do brilliant work. You can achieve anything. Nothing is too hard for you. You can get to the places of which you have dreamt. Others might have told you that it is difficult, but you do not have to listen to them. Just go for it! You will see that you will be able to do it. You can do the star stuff, too.

As a unique person, you are able to achieve your potentials. There are lots of opportunities waiting out there for you. Always attach to things you enjoy in life. Going for things you enjoy will make great opportunities for you, and you will excel.

Great opportunities are the things that you find easy and that give you recognition. You should be recognised in life; you should not just stay where you are. On the other hand, others might find similar things hard. You are not an ordinary individual – you were made to be a champion. Some people feel they aren't very special because of the things they have been through in life. They feel they are nothing. They do not believe in themselves and have been used by others. That's not the way it should be. They were made to feel very special. You, too, are special.

Some people feel others are special, but they feel they themselves aren't special because of their current situations. Do not allow your current situation to give you a bad name, because you are not going to remain in it forever. You are going to give birth to something beautiful in your future.

In this world, you have unique abilities that will be known, and that will make you feel very special. You are not going to remain with that old, awkward feeling about yourself. Using your abilities is going to make you feel that you are very capable, and in turn you will feel very special. You are a surprise to this world.

Do you think you are very special? Do you feel very special? I want you to be honest with yourself. How do you feel about yourself? Do you think you are on this earth to go through terrible situations? Maybe you have positioned yourself in the wrong place because you don't feel very special. I want you to move out of that position today and step into the brand-new you. You are a very special person and you deserve to achieve great things in life. You deserve so much more than you are getting at the moment. You deserve to be the best. You deserve to have a name that is greater than others.

Having a feeling of being very special can make you celebrate yourself. You know that you are something, and you are going far in life. You are not just in the midst of people for the sake of it. You are there to be noted, and you stand as a vessel of excellence.

Not feeling special can leave you with a feeling of sadness and of sitting on the edge. Someone sitting on the edge is unable to enter into good things. I want you to enter into good things and enjoy the very best of your life. It is very possible for you.

It is not a good thing to feel that you are not special. It's good to have a high self-esteem and a sense of satisfaction about yourself. That's the reason why feeling very special is very important and relevant to your life. You are a star! Feeling special will enable you to face any situation in life; you will know your worth, and nothing will drag you down. You will be able to carry yourself, even in times when you could be feeling down. You will be on top of the world, and you will win.

Maybe someone in your life has been making you feel like you aren't special. I want you to ignore that person. The person does not feel very special about himself. You are a very special individual and are going to live excellently and successfully. Feeling very special will enable you to walk into places where great things aren't happening, and you can turn it into a great place. You will be someone that will make others say, 'Who is that? He is so different.' They will be shocked about the high level of change and performance you bring to the table.

There are people whose presence makes you feel very special. Note them and try and keep their company. Stay with them because they make you feel high, they make you feel at your best, they make you feel strong and on top. That's very good, because you are amazing.

I have seen very special people being treated like nothing. They have allowed people to bring them down; they have been brainwashed by the lies and the wickedness of this world. They have allowed others to leave them feeling empty. Do not allow yourself to fall into such a trap, because you are remarkable. You do not have to live under the manipulation and suggestion of others. You can live your life to the best by making your own decisions as a very special person. You can choose what you want to do, and you do not have to depend on people's view before making your decisions. You are astonishing.

Feeling very special can make you fly high and can help you to rise towards great heights. It can help you do things that will amaze others. You can achieve it because your special abilities give you the ability to go higher and bigger.

You can live a life of feeling very special by treating yourself right and by placing attention on the things that improve your happiness. Get rid of the people that discourage you; don't allow anyone to put you down. Your duty is always to carry yourself up. You are incredible. Feeling very special will help you to live a life of greatness. You will not settle for less and will go for the things that are bigger and stronger. You will achieve them through your focus, and you will be satisfied and filled with a sense of being worthy, even in the midst of others.

People often focus too much on their problems and do not give themselves the space and the intellect to think that they are special. They allow their problems to speak bad things into their lives. Do not allow your problems to keep you in hiding from your destiny, because you are very special. When you find yourself in situations that do not make you feel special, say to yourself, 'I am very special and wonderful. This problem is only a sign of my greatness. I know that in my future, very special things are going to happen to me.'

Do not allow others to make you lose your sense of feeling special. Remember, people will always be around you, and the way they live their lives is entirely up to them. They might speak bad things to you; you simply have to keep yourself high and maintain your class. You are very special.

Some people are afraid to let other people know that they are special. They allow others to treat them poorly, and they end up carrying loads of negativity that do not belong to them. You have to exclude yourself from being part of things like that. You are here in life to feel special about yourself. You want a meaningful life; you want a life that tells you good things about yourself. You want to feel good every day of your life. You want to feel like you are somebody. Therefore, start feeling very special.

Maybe you are thinking about how you are going to start feeling special about yourself. Maybe you have been through too much and feel like it is not worth another day. I want you to know that you have to start thinking right about yourself. Dress great and do great things, because that's the start of you feeling special.

Let me give you a key for feeling very special. Always look into the mirror when you wake up and say to yourself, 'This great person that I am looking at in the mirror is going to be the very best today. I am going to be on top, and I am going to shine today.'

Even bad people can feel like they are special. They tend to have more boldness than others and be stronger. So why would a good person like you not feel very special about yourself? Start feeling special about yourself, because you are worth it.

I know a young girl that always feels very special. Anytime I see her, I see the best of the best. She is always happy, cheerful, and sharp. She does not like people speaking bad things towards her, and she always fights for her rights. She is an example of how people should feel.

If you are in a place where everyone is feeling very special, but you feel like you are the odd one out, what is stopping you? What do you see those people doing that make them feel special? Do the same thing and start feeling special about yourself. Do not allow your weaknesses to stop you from feeling special, because from the day you were born, you were already very special. You have been chosen to carry out a specific assignment (destiny) on this earth. Do you believe that? You are extraordinary!

If you stay in environments where people do not feel very special about themselves, and you are feeling the same way, then you have to move out of that environment and identify what is very special about you. Satisfying yourself is an important key to feeling special. You have to make sure that the things you do every day are the things you want to do; that brings a sense of satisfaction. You have to make sure that you please yourself, not others; by doing so you will feel very special.

Enjoying your life is also another important key to feeling very special. You cannot just live life without enjoying the moments – you have to laugh and make fun. You must always bring the best out of your day that makes you feel happy and fulfilled. Being able to do what you want is another key. You have to go to the places you want to go, fulfil the dreams you want to fulfil, celebrate yourself in the way you want, and make the plans you want. No one was created to control your life. You are in charge.

Sometimes you need to think that you are a very great person. You have to believe you are worthwhile, and you have to think of yourself as on a new level. You have to think of yourself going higher than your peers. By thinking so, you become it. You are very wonderful, so you have to believe it.

Once you are contented with your achievements, you have peace, and that is a reason to celebrate yourself.

Chapter 9
You Are Contented

It's a great thing to know that you are happy with where you are now. You must be satisfied with yourself, and you have to be pleased about your current state no matter how you wish things could be better. I know it's a great thing to wish for more, but you have to say to yourself, 'I am happy with where I am, and I will produce more to make a better future.'

Be content about where you are now, but be excited for the future. Don't wish to be like others. An individual that is not content compares himself to others. You do not need to compare yourself with others in any way. Try not to compare yourself with others, because you must remember that there are things you are good at that they are bad at. Not being content means you do not understand you're unique. You have to know that you *are* unique. You are the best of your kind.

Each individual carries something unique that can't be found anywhere else. Despite your inability to be able to make things better in your past, you still have to be happy and know that what you have done is the best of your effort. You have done what you can. Contentment also connects with understanding your opportunities. Every individual sees an opportunity in a different way. An opportunity becomes golden when it connects to what you enjoy. If you don't like the thing, there is no point going for it. Your golden opportunities stir up your passion. You are able to achieve your best as long as you recognise your golden opportunities, which are the things that you are able to do at your best level. You have a dream regarding them, and you aspire to see yourself there.

Be content with your past opportunities. Do not regret the things that you have not been able to achieve in the past. Do not try to adjust yourself to be like others; you can never be like them. Love yourself for what you have done and be grateful about your own opportunities. You are yourself and also your best, so be happy about it. Get rid of negative emotions that disturb you and make you look back. Build a peace of mind that is great, and make efforts to ensure nothing bad mixes it up. Stay clear and do not allow any storm to make you feel regret.

One of the reasons why having peace of mind helps you to celebrate yourself is because you will not be moved by the things of the world. No matter what is going on, you won't allow the things that glitters to make you lose your worth.

You would not say to yourself, 'I wish I can have what my friends have. I wish I could be like her one day.' That is deceit. You do not know the problems that are behind your friends' successes, and that is why you should not have to wish to be like them. Some people *look* all right, but they aren't all right inside.

Do not allow bad feelings to steal away the greatness of your day. You do not have to feel small because of the imperfections in your past. You must feel the greatness within you. You have to feel like someone that is going somewhere in life and who has goals.

You should always forgive yourself because it builds your contentment. You do not have to remember what has gone wrong in your yesterday; it should not cover your heart and disturb you from achieving new things. There is a lot for you to achieve today, and that's the great news. Just let it go and say, 'I am too happy to remember what happened in my yesterday.' Yesterday is gone and today is a new day. No more thinking and stressing yourself. No more going through the pain of the things that haven't worked out.

Try not to think too much about things that have not worked out. We all have things that haven't worked out in our past despite our efforts. You do not have to worry about it. However, you could repair it in the future. You can do better in the future.

You should keep your thinking clear and encourage good things in your thinking. You will not be able to enjoy life well when you are thinking too much of bad things. Be happy, be joyful, be glad, be cheerful, and be content with what you have done in life.

Thinking too much can make you anxious about the future. Always remember that the future will take care of itself. You don't have to ponder about the future too much; just leave it, and it will work out for your good. Meditate on how you have tried to make things work out in the past. You are appreciated for every time you try. Focus on the things you have done and embrace yourself. Be content about your productivity, and be proud to share it with others.

You do not have to force yourself to make things happen; you simply need to try a bit. Every trial you make is not a waste. It is a great effort to try something. When you try, you should appreciate yourself and feel good about what you have done. You should be pleased even if others aren't.

Be content about where you are today, because life goes in stages, and the stage you are in today is not where you will be in the future. You will overcome what you are going through today. There is still a lot of time for you to learn and grow. There is still time for the best in you to come out. Try to make yourself comfortable where you are. You don't have to live life feeling miserable and uncomfortable. Deal with whoever that is making you uncomfortable. Be a king where you are, and make sure you are doing what you want.

There is nothing wrong in soothing yourself. You don't have to satisfy others while leaving yourself feeling bad. You should make the best for yourself today and hope that tomorrow will be brighter. You have to give yourself the pleasure and excitement your life is looking for. If you are feeling down and sad, it's time for you to come out of that feeling. It's time for you to know that sorrow does not belong to you. Evil feelings do not belong to you. You have to start living happy now, regardless of your experience, and know that there is something beautiful ahead of you.

Reassuring yourself is also a key that leads to contentment. You have to tell yourself. 'It will be okay, it will be all right. Things are going to get better, and the sun is going to shine again.' How mighty you will feel when you start speaking such great words into your life!

People should see you as a calm person. No matter how violent the storm you are going through, you should remain relaxed and cheerful. Do not be moved by what is going on; keep your mind focused on enjoying your life, and allow your beauty of living a great life to flow.

You have to relieve yourself of the feeling that you have to fulfil the expectations of people. You don't have to do what they want or give them everything for which they are asking. You simply have to focus on yourself and make each day worth self-celebration.

Make sure you treat yourself in the best possible way. You know you are a very special person. You have been created to enjoy your life and not to suffer in this world. You are here to become the very best you want to be. Therefore, treat yourself very well and think highly of yourself.

Patience is a friend of contentment. You should be patient so that things can work out for the future. The good you do today might not bring results today, but in the future it will make a difference. Keep dong the good things you do, because they will bring reward with time.

Take things easy with yourself. You don't have to rush or make rash decisions. You don't have to solve all your problems in a day. Don't allow people to push you and stress you. A contented person does not feel insecure. Don't allow yourself to have insecurities. You don't have to be shy and timid because of the things you haven't yet achieved. You have to lift your head up high and know that confidence is your portion.

When people feel uncertain about the future, they aren't content; their eyes look here and there. They keep on asking people questions, and they keep wandering whether something good will come to them. You don't have to feel this way. You should be assured, and things will be well with you.

Don't feel shaky, and don't allow people to use you. Don't let them push you here and there, and don't go round in circles trying to do things in order to avoid the bad situation you are currently going through. Give yourself peace of mind, settle down where you are, and enjoy your now. Sometimes things don't work out because it is not the right time. You must hold on until the right time comes. You don't have to stress yourself. You don't have to feel troubled, and you don't have to be hard on yourself. Some people aren't content but feel others are. When they look at others they, see the things they have, and they focus on what looks big in the lives of others. They think others are better than themselves. They think others have done better. That's not true. In this world, there are people that look successful but aren't content on the inside. They keep blaming themselves and feel like they are the odd one out. They feel very ashamed to talk about the things they have done. Please do not find yourself in the same shoes.

Do you think you are content? Are you happy for who you are? Do you feel that you are outstanding? Whether you believe it or not, you *are* outstanding. You should never look down on yourself or feel as if there is something you have to achieve in order to feel better. You are content because you have great goals for your future, and you are going to make things happen. You are going to change from a negative attitude to a positive one. Taking positive actions in your future ensures that you get positive results.

Not feeling very contented can leave you with a lack of respect for yourself. As a human being, you have to respect yourself and carry yourself with dignity. You have to know that you deserve the best only, and that you will sail through life's difficulties like a champion. Maybe someone in your life has been making you feel uncomfortable, and it makes you feel you haven't done well. You can do your best to move out of the person's environment or ignore the person whenever he is around. You need to realise that there is no one that can do what you have done better than you.

Maybe you like helping people, but the people you are helping aren't satisfied with what you have done; they keep on complaining. You should stop helping them because you have done your best. Don't believe the negative things they say to you. There are people that are used to telling you the things you haven't achieved in life; maybe your parents fall into that category. Remember that there is nothing you can do about the past. The past remains as it is, but you do not have to lose your joy by looking back and feeling bitter.

I have seen very content people live very happy lives. They haven't allowed themselves to be affected by what others say. They know that their future will be brighter, and they don't even tolerate the presence of people that make them feel worthless and sad.

It's not a good thing to have a lack of contentment; it can leave you hopeless and down. That lack can make you struggle when you are meant to enjoy your life. It can keep you going round in circles and feeling like you have to find a solution. Maybe you are thinking of how you are going to start feeling contented. You simply have to start by smiling at yourself and believing you have done the right things in the past. Believe you will experience the rewards in your future.

Excellence and self-celebration are friends
because excellence brings satisfaction.
Then self-celebration happens.

Chapter 10
You Are Aiming for Excellence

You should celebrate yourself because you are aiming for excellence. Excellence is the ability to follow a path towards perfection. A person aiming for an excellent spirit has no choice but to celebrate himself. This kind of person is deserving in the eyes of others. There is no one that doesn't love excellence. In life, we all aim for excellence. You should celebrate yourself because you are also aiming for excellence. You are trying to improve from your position of yesterday, and this is greatly appreciated. You should feel good about it.

Keep aiming for excellence, because there are people watching you, and when they need you, they will show up. Your desire for excellence gives them a reason to celebrate you. Your excellence will also connect you with them: people will look for you when you are excellent.

However, excellence starts little by little, with a desire.

You have to desire it first, then make an effort, and then make changes in the areas in which you aren't performing well. You cannot be excellent in everything, but you can be excellent in the areas of your gifts and talents. Whenever you try, you've got it right. At the same time, you do not have to feel bad if you aren't excellent today. You are in the process of achieving it, and you will get there. Time appreciates you, and soon you will become better as you practise more. The golden side of you will come out, and you will be appreciated by this world.

You do not have to listen to the judgement of others when you are trying to achieve excellence. Remember, it's a process – and even they themselves have areas in their life on which they need to improve, so people should mind their own business. They should not focus on your own area that lacks excellence. Keep pressing on, and you'll get there. You are a very great individual. You will be satisfied when you do things in a very good way. You will not look at what others have, and you will know that you are the best of your kind. You will know that you are very good at what you do. You will be very pleased with yourself. You will not be moved by what others do. If you know that you are excellent, keep on going, because there is a lot of success ahead of you.

In life, you will often be in the midst of people, so you have to be prepared to make sure that you produce the best possible results at whatever you do. You have to be ready for excellence. Excellence can never erase you from the place you are; it will only spell your name bigger. Excellence will enable people to call out your name on the street and choose you amidst others. In the midst of your opponents, you will be able to win because you are excellent. You will be the choice of people because of your excellence. Excellence will make you the favourite of the world and will lift you up in your position in life. Excellence will make others to seek your help, which in turn increases your pride. It will make others desire to be like you. Excellence will make you flexible and adaptable in any situation. You will be able to change and make necessary adjustments when difficulties come. You will be able to move on swiftly with excellence.

Excellence will make you the pride of the world and will take you to the front while others are sitting at the back. Excellence keeps you on top, defines your purpose, and makes people not take you for granted. There are so many things in life that you cannot control, but if you desire excellence, you will be comfortable even when the worst things happen.

There are so many demands placed on you in life, but if you're excellent, you will not be moved. Excellence will help you say to yourself, 'I know my purpose, and nothing will easily move me.' When you add excellence to a meaningful activity, it becomes a success.

People will always remember you for excellence. Excellence enables you to leave a good impression. Excellence builds your self-trust and helps you to know that you have done your best. Excellence will prompt others to keep seeking you; they will have interest in you and will call you great.

Excellence gives you a lot to celebrate about yourself and helps you celebrate your good times. Excellence covers the area of your appearance, eating, career, goals, dreams, relationships, destiny, words, good deeds, habits, attitudes, and passions. Give excellence to all things. Excellence gives you the confidence to rest. You can easily have a break to relax and have some fun when you are excellent. Later on, you return back to your work. You know that the world is on your side because of your excellence. People will keep being attracted to you because you are excellent. Excellence helps you take your expectations seriously meaning you expect great results. If you are an excellent person, you will not expect any result – you will have high standards. You will expect the best, and you will not tolerate average of any kind.

With excellence, you can embrace where you are with joy. Excellence brings you satisfaction and happiness. You will say, 'I have performed to my best yesterday. Therefore, something very great is coming my way.' You will be delighted with yourself due to your excellence. You will hold on to where you are with great joy, and you will feel very good about yourself.

Excellence is a source of pleasure. It is very enjoyable, and life is enjoyable anytime you hold up to excellence. You will be filled with so much happiness and a sense of being worthwhile. You will look up high and will dance, because you know that your work of excellence has given a good account of you. Even behind your back, people will praise you because of your excellent spirit.

Excellence gives you power and makes you rule amidst people. If you are excellent, you will be a leader and will be in the forefront. You will be the one controlling how things should be. You will sit in the high places, and you will be asked for your ideas and intelligence, because of your excellent spirit.

Excellence will draw a fortune of good things into your life.

From all the sides of the earth, you will be asked for if you are excellent. People will be attracted to you, and nations will want to hear from you. People will be blessed by the work of your hands. They will want to know what is on the inside of you, and they will want to understand how you think.

Excellence makes you wiser than those that ignore it. Some people ignore excellence because they do not understand the power it carries; they do not have the example of excellent people in their lives, and they end up living ordinary lives. Please don't be part of that. You can be excellent. Excellence takes you far while others are left behind. You may have the gift of making something; add excellence to it, and you will make a fortune. You will be able to achieve higher things in your life because of your excellence. You will be able to get to places that others call difficult.

You might be acting excellently, but things are not working, and you wonder why. Don't worry – your time will come, and you will soon get noticed. It is never too late for you. It's not over – you are just about to begin. One day your name will be announced to all because of your excellence. Through you, a lot of good things can happen. Through your excellence, a lot of good things can be identified, which will make others celebrate you. Excellence makes you to go deeper into things and come out stronger. It will make you discover things about yourself which will wow others.

The things you have done in the past might be good, but with excellence you can do better. You can press forward and move on to the next level. You can do greater things that are beyond your mind. You can do amazing things in your life! There are priceless seeds of greatness inside of you: abilities, talents, gifts, and skills which might look small but produce excellence. You simply have to discover them and use them as an opportunity to reach out to others in an excellent manner, celebrating yourself at the same time.

You can live a life of excellence by waking up every day with the thought that you are going to reach out with your gifts and talents in an excellent manner. You are going to do what you haven't done before. You are going to show the world that you are the best. You should make others look for you by making sure that you do things in a fine way. You should leave everything that you touch in great condition. The work of your hands should bring a fine result. By doing so, you will be the centre of attention and investment for others.

You are in this world to excel and mount up with wings as eagles. Having wings mean preparing your life for greater things. You are here to fly and achieve all that you can. You aren't here to suffer; you are here to give your best to each day. You are not someone that deserves little things – the big things are for you. You are going to use your gift of excellence to do something great.

You don't have to live under people that will not allow you to use your excellent spirit. You do not deserve people who like to frustrate others and keep them away from achieving their full positions. Stay in environments that enable you to be excellent. It's not a good thing to feel unappreciated for your act of excellence. If you are excellent but do not feel rewarded in the place you are located, look for another environment where you will be picked out for your excellence. Your excellence is meant to connect you with kings and great people. Your feeling of being excellent can make you shine and come out very strongly. It can help you to conquer areas of your life where you feel little. It can help you to rise up and become one of the very best, setting you up for greatness.

Knowing you are excellent will help you to run your race until you win. It will help you to set yourself apart for something special, treating yourself like a king or queen.

You will not live an ordinary life when you are excellent – you will live an extraordinary one.

When you find yourself in situations where you aren't allowed to use your excellence, or you feel undermined despite your excellence, you don't have to worry. As long as you feel you are doing the right thing, keep pressing on, and you will witness your excellence draw people to you. Do not allow what others do to make you feel you aren't excellent. Excellence can never be missed in life. There are still people that will notice you, and if they have the bravery to tell you that you are excellent, they will. You should never feel a sense of regret or shame when you know that you have offered your best.

Recently people focus too much on their problems instead of celebrating their excellence. They are not even aware that they *are* excellent; they think they aren't good enough. They have tried in life, yet they can't celebrate the great things they have done through their excellence. I know a young boy that has an excellent singing spirit. He sings very well in a choir. Everyone enjoys his voice, and even his singing mates know that he is very good. However, the choir leader doesn't give him the opportunity to lead songs. Regardless, the boy is very happy and keen.

Do not allow your weaknesses to stop you from aiming

towards excellence. Your mind might say to you, 'You haven't done anything right in the past. Even the one time you tried yesterday, no one liked you for it.' You don't have to allow your mind to deceive you. Keep striving for excellence. Don't allow anyone to frustrate your excellence. You might be doing the right thing, while the idle people keep picking on you. They have nothing to add to what you are doing, but they want to say something negative in order to discourage you. Don't mind them, because they can't win.

I want you to always appreciate yourself in life, and appreciate every step you take in order to be excellent. Excellence is going to make you into a big person. It won't leave you at the back; it will take you to the highest points, from where you will lead forever.

If you make an advance in the areas of your dreams, you will meet unexpected success on the way. If you have decided to live an excellent life, I can assure you that you will meet something good on the way; you will achieve your goal and even possibly go beyond it. Success is not scarce in your life; it lies in your hands, and you are going to achieve it.

I am sure that you have a specific picture of the type of the life you want. As you add excellence to everything you do, you will see that your imaginations will become a reality, and you will walk in high places. You will get to places that are beyond your imagination, and you will be a clear and typical example of success in this world.

I encourage you to keep following your heart and put the best into everything upon which you lay your hands. You will see that things will not turn out to be failures. They will work out to your advantage and will bring goodness into your life. Your life will be very outstanding when you are mindful of the excellence in all you do. You will be raised up through excellence. Excellence can never make you small; instead, it turns you into a huge person. When you are excellent, you will wake up to see that life has a lot in store for you. You will taste things that you have not tasted before. You will walk into blessings that you haven't walked into before. You will walk with people that you have not walked with before. You will wake up to see that you are not in this world to suffer; you are here to enjoy life. Start adding excellence to the things you do.

An excellent spirit will enable you to discover your place in life. You are not here to toil and suffer rejection. When you add excellence to the things you do, you will sit down like a king. You will be ruling and will not be under people. Excellence will bring out the originality of your nature and destiny.

You have a vision in life regardless of your past or the

current circumstances that surround you. Your vision is very precious, and you will achieve it using your gifts and talents. Where do you see yourself in five years' time? What would you love to be doing in five years? That is your vision. When you add excellence to your vision, you become a very sharp element that removes old things. Everything you experience will be new, and you will feel very blessed. Your life will be filled with precious gifts.

I want you to believe in yourself. Always see the possibility that lies within every talent and gift that you have. See the possibility that you are able to get something out of your situation. See the possibility that your gifts and talents can take you to a high place. You are able to do a lot more in life, so open your eyes wide and visualize yourself climbing high, even in places that most people do not reach. You are not here to achieve average; the best is for you. Therefore, be sharp to view opportunities in every place you go.

Your dreams are not going to be cast away; they will become a reality one day. You will reach the place of which you have always dreamt. You also will sit in high places. You are not a small individual, and your life is guaranteed to bring you success and good fortune. You will see that you are drawing closer to your dreams every day that you act out with an excellent spirit. Your good attitude is going to pay off and bring blessings your way.

It's never too late for you. You aren't done yet – there are beautiful colours waiting for you in your future. There are wonderful things that life has in store for you. You are going to be excellent and reach great heights. The impossible shall become possible for you. You are going to win and will not be cast down. You are going to fly high. Say to yourself, 'I am going to build great plans. I am going to think of great ideas that I can use to advance myself. I am not going to settle for less – I am stepping up.' Never stop planning for greatness. It will count in the future. Even if one plan does not come out as you expect, the other ones will bring you something good.

Do not allow anything to kill the fire that you have towards your dreams and visions. Keep the passion going and focus on your interests. Do not let anyone put you down. Don't let anyone talk you out of your dreams and visions. Remember that they belong to you, and you have the right to protect them from evil people that can destroy them. Keep up your enthusiasm. Keep aspiring for great things in life. The great things you are thinking of will bring you honour one day, leading you to meet people that are very great. You will be proud that you kept on dreaming. Keep up the excitement regarding the great things that you are expecting for your life. Remember, it starts inside of you! As long as you have it inside you, it will come out one day.

You should celebrate yourself even when things do not work out in your own time, because you know it's probably not the right time yet.

Chapter 11
You Understand and Flow with Timing

There is a time for everything in life. Everything is not going to work out today, probably because the time is not yet. When the time comes, it will work out, and you are going to be very happy. Don't be frustrated when it looks like you are pushing the right buttons but the doors aren't opening – the doors will open in the future. Others will celebrate you when your time comes. A person that does not understand timing will struggle in life. I do not want you to struggle. I always say to myself that if I do something and it doesn't work, maybe it is not the right time for it. There is a time for everything. When the time comes, it will work for me.

Some people think that everything will work out today. They want it to work out right now, and if it doesn't, they bang their heads against the wall. Things work out little by little and it often takes time. No matter how long you have been waiting for something to work out, celebrate yourself regardless; it will still work out. You are worthy of being celebrated.

There is a time to labour, and there is a time to gain. You might be working hard today but not getting enough results. Don't worry about it, because you are preparing for your future. The effort you are making counts towards your future. All the effort you have made throughout your life will benefit you in your future. Life works with time; it is very natural, and that is how life works. You are not going to break down – you are going to become a success. You are a winner in the process. The fact that things don't work out now does not mean that you should break down. Keep going, because every effort counts. In the future, things will turn out nicely, and you will celebrate.

Sometimes you can feel tired of running your race because things aren't working out, but I assure you that you will be a winner. It is not about now; it is about your future. You are going to win in the future. Your tomorrow will be better. You are going to be a leader in your race, so do not be tired and do not give up. Take your eyes off your current sufferings. The fact that the time for you to be big isn't yet here doesn't mean you were born to suffer. Your success is in the future. People will be surprised of what you will become. You are not going to give up. You are going to climb upwards and overcome your challenges so that your beautiful side will show. You are going to make it. I will see you make it, and I will celebrate you.

Life works with time, and you are going to become somebody important one day. Don't allow others to deceive you, and don't put your head down. Don't feel as if you are the odd one out. Something will turn out in your favour when your time comes. You will be a leader in the forefront, and your success will be apparent from all angles. Every difficulty you are facing now is not going to be the same come tomorrow. Those difficulties are going to be over. I know you are going through lots of challenges at the moment, but it is not the end of the world for you – it's the beginning for your greatness. The best things are coming out of your tomorrow. You are going to make it through; all you need is to take things one step at a time.

You might be down today, but that doesn't mean you will be down forever. You will climb higher; you will even achieve more than others who have gone ahead. Your life is going to make sense. Your life is a very bright one, and you will come out winning on the other side. You simply have to enjoy the time you have now, and allow the time for other things to come. Look for new things to do and enjoy yourself. Why do you think you are enjoying one or two things at the moment? It is because you are in the proper time for it. The fact that you are enjoying what you are enjoying today means that there are new things that will come into your life in the future. Just wait for the right time.

Waiting for the right time to come does not mean that it's over; it doesn't mean it will never work out. It doesn't mean you aren't going to be fulfilled in life. The better things will come to you; you simply have to understand the principle of timing so that you have some peace in your mind. Waiting for the right time prepares you to handle what is coming your way and makes you grow with maturity. It makes you a better person and develops your attitude, helping you to build skills for handling people. Imagine giving a management job to a boy of sixteen years. One should understand that his maturity cannot be compared to that of a twenty-eight-year-old. The twenty-eight-year-old has learnt more in life and would have more experience in handling people compared.

A winner is a champion after going through the odds. You have to go through difficult times to be a spectacular person. I want you to look on the inside of yourself, particularly at the good things about yourself. Every good thing you've done is useful. The world will be proud of you and will lift you up for celebration. It's not over yet because you are very special. You are going to be very successful because you are in the preparation stage. In life, we all have to prepare for things. The time you are in now gives you the chance to prepare yourself well and to learn lessons that will benefit you before your next promotion. Promotion comes after you have passed the test of time.

Therefore, don't waste time – don't waste today! Use it very well and start making improvements to your life. Build your character, your confidence, your skills, and your intelligence so that you will be able to excel when you earn a bigger position. I know you desire bigger things in your life, and your desire will become a reality very soon.

Time allows you to learn lessons. The time of 2014 will enable you to learn new things and gain new ideas that will help you to excel in 2015. That's why you shouldn't take anything for granted. What you are going through now will train you to handle things in the years to come. You will become a better person and will enjoy your victory very well.

You don't have to live under people that do not give you the opportunity to grow. Imagine a mother that expects a baby to grow on the day it is born. Everybody will say that the woman has no understanding. You need to stay with mature people that can tolerate your mess until the time comes for you to mature yourself and become someone greater. A person that can tolerate your nonsense is a very nice person; he or she will allow time to mature you.

Do not stay in environments where you feel pushed to do things despite knowing they aren't working. You have to be strong and believe in yourself. Say to yourself, 'Everyone can be rushing, but I am going to wait right here until my time comes. I am not going to be worried because it hasn't worked out today. I know it will work out in time.' You may not know it but you can give your best in the time you are now. You can live in the moment and enjoy what is around you, regardless of how small it may be. You can tune into the enjoyment of life and enjoy what life has to offer you. You can add laughter, which brings you energy. You can be free. Enjoy yourself even in the bad and terrible seasons, because you know that a change is on the way.

Your preparation will be a success and will make your future look very good. You are on this earth to make a difference that will shake the world. What is in you is different. Do not be afraid of the outside world when stepping into your opportunities. There are many opportunities waiting for you, and you are going to use them to wax strong and become a more intelligent person.

Things work with time. You might get some things done today, but you might have to leave some for tomorrow. The things that do not work out today may work out tomorrow. Allow time to work things out for you. You don't have to force it. When the time comes, it will get better; when one door closes, another one will open.

You cannot fully understand how life works. Sometimes you do a good thing but get no results; however, that does not mean it will not work out one day. If you notice, people that get results are those who have laboured seriously in the past. It looked like they were going nowhere, but when they waited patiently, they eventually got a result. You will get great results, too, and you will be an example.

There is a time to make sacrifices, but when the right times comes, you will benefit because you have already sacrificed in the past. Don't worry when the sacrifices you make do not bring a good result your way; remember that you have done your part, and when the right time comes, you will benefit. After every pain, there is always a gain. You *will* gain.

I know there are a lot of good things that are about to come into your life because of the sacrifices you have made in the past. I understand that life is not easy, but I can assure you that you will still be successful when the time comes. You aren't going to remain where you are forever. You will move forward and will always remember to celebrate yourself.

There is a time to plant, find, save, keep silent, and go to war. On the other hand, there is a time to reap, benefit, and give. Whatever time you are experiencing, enjoy yourself, because that's the best you can give to yourself. I know that you are experiencing some difficulties in your life, but I want you to remember that you are a star in the making. Don't let anything stop you from enjoying your life. You might be suffering today from financial difficulties, sickness, parental issues, or loss. Your bad situation will not last forever. The darkness you are experiencing will turn into light one day. One day things are going to turn around and work out for your good.

Understanding timing will make you relax. You do not have to be where your friends are, but you also don't have to compare yourself to them; be grateful for where you are. You might be celebrating others today, but when your time comes, they will celebrate you, and you will celebrate yourself.

Babies do not crawl the same time day they were born. Their mother knows that there is a time that the babies start crawling, and they patiently wait for that time to come. Wait for your time, too. Don't go forward and make rash decisions. Don't hit your head against the wall because things aren't going your way. Soon your life will be stunning.

You might be studying now and not have money to buy yourself good things. The time to earn money will come, and you will be working soon. You will have lots of money when the time comes. Your situation is not going to be same as others. You are going to win, and you will walk on the road called success. Sometimes you might knock on a door, and it doesn't open; that does not mean no door will open in the future. Your investment is not going to be a waste. I know a friend who had a business, but there was a time where the business wasn't working; now it is very successful. My friend waited. You must also wait for your time to come. Assuming she had given up then, I wonder about the loss. There would be nothing to gain.

I also have a friend that went to university with a number of qualifications. After finishing her studies, she could not get a job for the first five years, but later she got a job. You will receive a miracle, and a change will come your way.

139

Believe me, there are greater things ahead of you. Do not say bad things to yourself because your timing is early. There is a difference between right timing and early timing. Early time is when you go ahead of time and then don't get the results you expect. Right timing is when you do it in a time whereby that timing brings a result.

It is normal to be in a position of early timing because we all feel we should do things, and we try our best. However, we have to wait for the right timing, which refers to when we will get our results. Take life easy. Something that seems to come late doesn't mean it will never come.

You are in life to maximise your time. You are here to give the best to yourself all the time. You don't have to worry, and neither do you need to be afraid. You should always look up. You have to be proud of yourself. Others might be in their time because things are working for them, but that doesn't mean it won't work out for you.

There are people whose presence will make you feel inferior. They will make you feel down because things aren't working out for you. They want you to sort out your life. They are tired of helping you and make you feel discouraged because they do not understand that your time hasn't come yet. Don't stay near people like that.

Let me give you a key for enjoying your time. Stand on your feet and believe in yourself. Don't allow things that glitter like gold to make you feel down because you don't have them. Remain balanced and keep your joy. Keep going, keep enjoying, and keep waxing stronger. You are truly great.

Understanding timing will enable you to arise and live to your best. It will help you to ignore those things that aren't working out for you. It will help you to keep focused on the good things that are going on in your life, giving you a healthy mind.

You should see your mistakes as opportunities; this will fill you with self-celebration.

Chapter 12
You See Your Mistakes as Opportunities

Your mistakes are normal, because very successful people today have made mistakes in the past. They are still making mistakes, but you may not be able to see them. Don't allow your mistakes to bother you. The last thing you should think is that your mistakes will affect your future. Don't think that way. You will grow into success. Mistakes are part of the learning process of life. Your mistakes should not shock you; instead, they should remind you that you will get it right the next time. Some people cry and feel unhappy when they make mistakes. Don't cry, because your destiny is more special than your mistakes. The place you are going is ahead of you, and you will shine greatly when you get there.

You should think more about the good things you have done in life. Anyone can make a mistake; anyone can fall.

Believe in yourself even when you make mistakes, and remember you are on top. Always celebrate your success and look for something good to celebrate in your life.

Mistakes cover anything, including addictions. Give yourself the room to think of new things and make use of every minute. What do you do after making a mistake? You just have to move forward. There is a lot of fun and pleasure you can add to your life instead of thinking of your mistakes. I know you will grow up one day and overcome those addictions and mistakes.

Your mistakes do not mark the end of life – mistakes are the beginning of greatness. A great person is someone that has made mistakes before. No one is going to kill you because you made a mistake. Don't get down on yourself because you have made a mistake. Don't belittle yourself or consider yourself as unworthy. It is not over, because you have passion for what you do, and you will not repeat that mistake again. Next time you will be better and even possibly the best. Your mistakes make you a star because they give you creative ideas about how to make changes. We all make mistakes because they are part of life. Do not have regret because of your mistakes; don't keep on thinking about them.

The wrong thing you did yesterday has passed, and there

is no reason to remember it anymore. Mistakes come from weaknesses. You might not be strong in a specific area and produce a bad result, but don't give up. You are still good in other areas. You are excellent and beautiful. You are on top.

My mistakes do not keep me from trying again. They do not make me feel down. After making a mistake, I feel comfort in myself, but I remind myself that I will not repeat it. I still rise up to do what I want to do. I still produce my best, and there is no reason for me to regret anything. Mistakes do not make me feel ashamed. I cannot remember the mistakes I made four or five years ago. I know I am not where I was 5 years ago. I know I should be moving forward and making great plans for my life. I am not a small person – I am a big person.

You can change from making mistakes little by little. It doesn't happen all at once; it takes time, and it is very important for you to understand that. It takes time to drop a bad habit. Your friends might have dropped theirs, but it took them time to do so. It will also take time, and you will be proud of yourself very soon. You should believe that you are doing your best at the moment; don't be sad because others have gone ahead of you. You will still get there and will win against your problem.

The great thing is that you are willing to change. If you are willing to change, I celebrate you for that. There is no perfect man on the surface of the earth. You might be struggling to come out of some habits. Struggling is natural, but one day you will come out of that habit. You might have failed a thousand times, but your success is still assured.

We all want to be better human beings, and surely you will be better, too. You will change and will see yourself move from one level to the other. You should see your mistake as an opportunity, because it gives you the chance to grow.

Your mistakes make your life more beautiful and help you to be this awesome person whose story surprises others. When people look at you, they will not believe that someone like you will become so great and strong. Remember that your mistakes only make you into a stronger person. A lot of people say to themselves, 'I cannot do anything right.' You have to realise that you have done a lot of things right, but you have done a few wrong. There are a lot of perfections in you compared to your imperfections. Make sure you always recognise that.

Make it a goal to have peace about yourself and about where you are in life. There is no need to fight yourself and think you are not up to some standard. You do not have to be up to the standards of others in order to celebrate yourself. You can still live a life of self-celebration and shine just as you are.

Do not focus on your faults, because there is nothing much in it. A lot of people have faults, but it doesn't show on their faces; when you see them, they appear in their best. You can never know what they are struggling with on the inside. You do not know what is making them ashamed in their lives. I can assure you that they have faults, too. Your mistakes are not going to last forever. Build a life where you love yourself. You should wake up every day feeling interested in your day and in yourself. You should always do things that make you feel refreshed. You should have great and interesting plans.

Maximise how you enjoy your life. Get some pleasure going for you. Your mistakes should not stop you from enjoying life. They should make you enjoy it more, because you know a better you is on the way. You do not have to be disappointed about your mistakes or failures; you don't have to continue in self-pity. Self pity is not for you, and even people that have made worse mistakes do not dwell in pity. You should live your life to the fullest and let the best of you come out.

You can make a mistake because you had a need or you

were not informed about something. You can rush in your actions and make a mistake because you needed to take an immediate action. However, that happens sometimes in life. You don't have to be down because of your mistakes. Do not dwell on thoughts that are wrong. Don't dwell on thoughts that remind you of bad things in your past. You must know that you are a winner and are going to make it someday. You will be exalted in this world. You will run to the high places and will remain high forever.

There might be people coming your way that remind you of your mistakes. You simply have to get rid of them. Don't allow anyone to put you down or to win your day. Celebrate yourself and continue to do so. No one has the power to bring you down or prevent you from enjoying yourself.

Get rid of anything that reminds you of your mistakes – throw those reminders out of the window! You might be hearing voices that remind you of your mistake. Do not think that is the voice of God, because God does not have the time to speak of your mistakes. God is happy with you.

Your conscience can be fighting you as well, reminding you of your mistakes. You are free to do whatever you want to do in your life, and your conscience does not have the right to stop you. Your conscience is only deceiving you and trying to steal your joy. You have to step up and enjoy today, because it has the best in store for you. You should love yourself because the greatest love of all is the one you show yourself. You should give yourself the best and present the best to the world.

Don't continue talking about your mistakes; instead, talk positively. See things positively and don't listen to those who say negative things about you. Keep your mind positive and keep climbing higher. Talk to people about your victories instead of your mistakes.

Negative words are very destructive, so do not include them in your world. Every day of your life, say positive things about yourself. Say great things that will make you feel great. Develop relationships with people that speak good things into your life. Spend more time with people that make you feel good about yourself.

Find the things that make you happy and develop them. Do things that make you feel happy, and do not touch the things that make you sad. Let your life be a happy example. Build up good habits that make you happy. Always be happy, and don't allow the world to steal your happiness.

Your mistakes aren't going to be with you forever; they are simply going to be around for some time. Before you know it, you will be perfect. Therefore, enjoy your life despite your mistakes and know that you are a great person. You are going to do great things on this earth, and you will be remembered for them. Don't allow your mistakes to stop you from going for something. I see you as a perfect person, and there is a lot of capability inside you. You can do anything because the power lies within of you. Go for your dreams and leave no stone unturned.

If you are in a place where everyone is feeling bad because of their mistakes, know that you don't have to feel that way. You have a dream lying in front of you and are destined for great things. You have to stand out in the midst of the crowd and be courageous. Take the steps you want to take.

Do not allow your weaknesses to stop you from viewing yourself as a perfect person. You should view yourself as perfect because it is part of being a positive person. You have to believe you are what you hope you will become. You have to say it as if it has happened, even when it hasn't happened yet. Let me give you a key that will enable you to see your mistakes as opportunity: know that you have the power. You are powerful in a way that you can turn your mistakes into blessings. You simply have to push the excellence that is within you out. Show that you are very capable.

Some people feel they are making mistakes because they

are being directed by others. Do not allow people to direct your life. Live your life for yourself. Don't allow others to impose decisions on you, because you'll end up going for things that are not your interests. They are not in control – you are.

Don't be deceived by what looks perfect in the life of others; they have also fallen before. In fact, you will be surprised that you are even more capable than them. You have what it takes to be a perfect person.

In this world, you will not be beaten up for your mistakes. Instead, your mistakes will give you the opportunity to shine. Let go of your mistakes, because they will make you feel uncomfortable and irritated. Let them go because they will not add fun to your life. You are in this world to enjoy yourself.

Do you always think about your mistakes? What sort of mistakes do you think of? It is time to clear that away. There is a better person inside of you; you are a person of gold. There are treasures inside of you, and you are important. You are a source of happiness to this world, and I want you to realise that today. It's time for you to think of your bright side. Think about how intelligent you are. There is goodness inside of you, and there are lots of things in you that will bless others. Your life is going to erase the mistakes of others, and you will be a source of joy to them.

When you feel you have made a lot of mistakes, you will not have the boldness to face others. Don't feel the mistakes you have made yesterday; instead, sing a good song to yourself anytime you have feelings about your mistake. Remind yourself that you are greater than anything.

Maybe someone in your life has been talking about your mistakes. Maybe the person has been telling the world about how bad you are. I want you to know that you should not stand for that. You are going to become perfect. Your desire to become perfect will become a reality, and you will shine as the best. You don't have to judge yourself because of your mistakes. Don't put that load on your head. You won't feel light when you keep judging yourself. Instead, feel free and put your mistakes aside. Enjoy where you are and enjoy the process of perfection.

You are powerful as a human being, and that power makes you create what you want. Therefore, you can celebrate.

Chapter 13
You Are Powerful

As a human being, you are powerful. You are not just ordinary – you were made to do powerful things. If people have told you that you are not powerful, ignore their words. You have to believe in yourself and in your own power. You are a superior being, and you rule over animals, your environment, and plants. When you discover your destiny, you will see that the power to create beautiful things lies inside of you. You have the power to correct your environment and make things work out for you.

You should celebrate yourself because you are powerful. Do not undermine yourself or feel that there are people that can do things better than you. Your power will help you to stand high and overcome your challenges. Your performance will be high when you discover the power inside you. You have the power to go for what you want in life. You have the power to lead amidst others and not let them disturb you. Maybe you'll find yourself in a position where people are using you. You have to realise today that you have the power to change that.

You can come out of your hiding place. You can come out of your weaknesses and start operating in strength. You also have the power to deal with your enemies. Understanding the actions that can hinder self-celebration will help you deal with your enemies. Enemies are things or people that you do not find favourable. You have the power to create things and make things happen. Some people feel they aren't powerful because of their experiences in the past; the hurt they have been through and the fact that people have used them makes them feel inferior. Even if you have been used in the past, you are still powerful. Nothing should stop you from seeing yourself as a powerful person.

Some people feel that others are more powerful because they tend to have more things. They look successful and posh, and jealous types keep their eyes on the outward things that people have. You are a powerful person, and the day you realise that is when you will begin to enjoy your freedom. In this world, you are here to be powerful and to create the life that you want. You are here to grow as you want. You aren't a small person; you are mighty, and there are great deeds inside of you. You will not believe where you will get to in your future. You are going to achieve things that are beyond your imagination!

Do you think you are powerful? You have to know it for yourself; I cannot realise it for you. Do you feel powerful? You should feel powerful because no one is controlling your day. You are in charge of it. You can move to wherever you want. You are free to become whatever you want to be. You are powerful because you are on high. You aren't a wanderer on the surface of the earth. You have dreams inside of you, and you know exactly what you want to achieve. There is a desire in you to follow a specific path and become successful. You want to reach for what you want. Not feeling powerful can leave you with a feeling of emptiness. You can easily be tossed here and there if you do not feel powerful. You will not be able to stand your ground and keep your focus on the area in which you desire to shine.

Maybe someone in your life has been treating you poorly and controlling your life. It is time for you to come out of that situation. You have to say to yourself, 'I am not just an ordinary person – I am very powerful.' You must stand firm and remove yourself from situations like that. There are people whose presence can make you lose your power. They want you to be under them, and they don't want you to be free and happy. They want you to live a boring life. You don't have to stay around people like that. Keep far away from them.

Feeling powerful will enable you to have great plans for your life. You will be able to write out exactly what you want from life. You will be able to single yourself out amidst the crowd to live for your destiny. You will stand clear and be mindful of where you are going without distractions. I have seen powerful people living under people who dislike seeing them powerful. They get hooked with manipulative people that do not want them to live a fulfilling life. You don't have to get hooked into situations like this. You are free to be yourself and to control your world.

It's a bad situation if you do not feel powerful. You have the right to feel powerful and to live a powerful life. You are not here for others to rule over you and show you how to live your life. You have a lot of opportunity awaiting you that will help you to become a powerful person. Step into it! Feeling powerful can make you to live with high self-esteem. You can stand tall even when others are short. You can deal with your problems in a way that will not affect you negatively. You can live a joyful life and keep your smile even when others think you will not be able to withstand the problem.

When you find yourself in situations that make you feel weak, try to take charge again. Don't allow situations to control you and make you lead a miserable life. You are a very special person and do not deserve little things in this life. You deserve to be fully blessed and to enjoy life to the fullest.

Do not allow others to make you feel like you aren't powerful. There are people whose presence can be very annoying. You don't have to allow people like that to make you feel like you are beneath them. You do not have to be shy in their presence and hide your true nature. Show your nature to the world and shine wherever you are, regardless of the people around.

Lately people focus too much on their weaknesses and not enough on the fact that their strengths make them powerful. Always use your strength to rule in this world. Use your strength to create a big and precious life that you enjoy. You are here to take advantage of your day and use the resources around you to celebrate yourself. You are here to maximise every opportunity that comes your way; use them to show how awesome you are. Don't allow a day to go pass by without you utilising it.

Maybe you are thinking about how you are going to start gaining your power. You simply have to know who you are first and then realise the potential that is inside of you. You have to be in environments that make you mindful of the fact that you are a very special person. Use your talents; by so doing, you will feel powerful.

Let me give you a key for feeling powerful. Make sure you always dress great and take care of your appearance. When you start doing so, you will see that others will treat you in a special way. You will become a quality person in the eyes of others.

I know a young girl who is very powerful. She is always focused and doesn't let people waste her time. She is a manager at her workplace and doesn't give time for things that don't benefit her. She knows what she has on the inside, and she shows people that she is a very great person.

If you are in a place where everyone is feeling powerful but you are not, you do not have to worry. We cannot all be powerful in every way, but we do have areas in which we can be powerful as individuals. Focus on the area in which you are powerful and allow that to give you a boost and a sense of richness in every area of your life. You do not have to allow your weaknesses to stop you from using your power. You have the power to stop negative things from coming into your life. You have the power to build something special for yourself. You can live a great life despite your weaknesses. Don't allow your weakness to speak to you; instead, you should speak to your weaknesses.

If you stay in environments where people don't feel powerful, everyone is weak and helpless. You do not have to join them in feeling weak; simply stand out and exercise your rights. Don't allow the choice of the crowd to be *your* choice. Choose for yourself to be powerful, and you will be. Making use of your talents is also a key for feeling powerful. You can use the gift inside you to create a powerful world for yourself. Using your gifts will make you feel high and on top of the world. Your talents will make you very confident and useful in this world, so use them.

Being able to make positive decisions is another key to feeling powerful. As an adult you can decide for yourself where you want to go. As long as you are making positive decisions, no matter how small they are, you will still be powerful. Rule your life and don't allow others to control you. Sometimes you must remember that you are capable. You have to believe in yourself and shouldn't allow anyone to stop you from believing in yourself. No one has the power to stop you from using your capacities. You must think that you are capable in order to be capable. See yourself there first, and then you will be able to experience it.

A powerful person is very influential. Do not allow others

to influence you – instead, influence *them*. Lead others to where you are going and help them to understand you. Help them to see your dreams and go in the direction you want. It will save you a lot of time when you are influential. In a group, talk and try to influence the decision making. Don't hide your talents, and don't be shy. Come out and let them see who you truly are. You are more than able. You can influence the process of things, especially when you are involved. Your presence can be very powerful, to the extent that it will make your future bright. By being influential in your workplace, you also make a good future for yourself.

You are in this world to be a commander and not a follower. That's the reason why you must discover your purpose: you have to know what your purpose on this earth is. You have an assignment here that has to do with your destiny, which makes you a commander. In your destiny, you are a leader and others are your followers. Your helpers are your followers when it comes to your destiny.

Sometimes you have to give orders to people that are trying to disturb your life. They don't want you to fulfil your destiny, and you have to control them by giving them a warning. You should not let them waste your day by causing you to mess about. You don't have to give them the chance to waste time. You don't have to lose your focus in the process of dealing with them.

You are an important and powerful person. You are important because your presence is crucial. Your uniqueness is appreciated within a team. Your ideas are beautiful and help to smooth over problems. The things you have to say make great contributions and help to bring powerful changes. Your talents make you a leader. Therefore, nobody has the right to boss you around. You are a king in your own world; you are in charge of yourself. You have the power to construct your journey and bring the best out of it. You have the power to take charge anytime and stop negative things from happening to you. As a powerful person, you are able to organise yourself. You are able to make the wrong things right and to make decisions that will influence your day. You are able to organise things that will make your life more special and great. You are able to organise new things into your life that will make you feel more precious and valuable as a human being.

You are the head and not the tail. You are in front and not behind. You deserve the best, and no one has the right to mistreat you. You should know that for yourself. You are in this world to lead and sit in the front. You have the power inside of you to take yourself from the back seat; you are now in the front. You have to reach for the best.

In life, you can be a guide for others. You can be an example to others and allow your life to teach them how they should live their lives. You have what it takes to be seen as a great leader and to give guidance to others. You have the power to live a very successful life. Your life teaches others what to do when they face problems, because you have been able to properly handle your problems.

In your life, you can become whatever you want to become. You can become a principal, a director, a guide, a president, a supervisor, a controller, or a chief through your talents and by making great decisions for your life. You are not on this earth to be pulled here and there by people. You are here to be the light of the world. Therefore, do not hide the best that is inside of you – bring it out today.

You are the first and not the last. You must achieve this by starting to take great actions for your life and following the right path that will lead to your success. By doing so, your friends and family will begin to look unto you. They will respect you and call you good names. You were made to be the first, and you do not need to join the stragglers.

You deserve to come first in every area of your life. Your

life should mark the beginning of new things and should be fresh every day, because you practise self-celebration. You should run to the front and not stay at the back. By coming first, you will be a pride to the nation. Don't allow anyone to leave you at the back; instead, move forward. Your life is an original piece, and you are a great project of its own, so work on yourself. Specialise in making yourself better until you become the best. Keep moving forward and focus on achieving great things. Your talents make you a special person in the eyes of others; you are a very great person, and you have to believe that.

You can open a new chapter of your life today and start making use of the power inside of you. If you have not yet discovered the power you have, then start discovering it now. You can begin again and forget about the bad things in your past. You have the capability to step into a greater future by your actions.

Always think of yourself as powerful. You don't have to tolerate everything that comes your way; you can arrange and design something good to come your way. You can always expect greater things to come your way. There are treasures in this life that are meant for you; however, you will only enjoy them when you discover that you are a powerful person.

You have the right to say no to things you do not like. That's where your power comes in handy. You have the power to create powerful days for yourself. You can draw life and good things to yourself. You have no limitation. You are free to soar and become the greatest.

**The good self-image you possess will
create joy in you and will make it easy
for you to celebrate yourself.**

Chapter 14
You Have a Good Self-Image

Anyone with a good self-image can easily celebrate himself or herself. I want you to know that you are beautiful, and that can never change. External beauty is something that we all desire, but at the same time we need internal beauty. You have to believe that you are beautiful because when you first came to this world as a baby, everyone saw you as beautiful. Everyone received and welcomed you into the world. Why do you think that you are not beautiful? I know you might have doubts about your external beauty, but I want you to change them today. Believe in yourself!

Maybe people have told you that you do not look beautiful. Maybe someone said to you, 'You don't look good in that.' Forget about what people say. Most of them don't believe in themselves, so what's their business with yours? You are very beautiful, and your beauty is amazing.

Your external beauty is important and you do not have

to look like others. You can use makeup because it was created to enhance beauty. If you want to use makeup, use it in an excellent way and look great. There is nothing bad about makeup, but if you like to be natural, then be natural. Make your own choices and feel free to be yourself.

However, if you say you do not like how your face looks, something is wrong. I want you to start believing in yourself and change the negative thoughts that come to your mind regarding your external beauty. You are more than beautiful. You look great!

Your internal beauty is also there. You have great characteristics and abilities that make you beautiful on the inside. It is not every time that people look on the outside; sometimes they appreciate what is on the inside. What is on your inside makes you great and puts you on top in life. For example, say you are going for a job interview, and they ask you questions, but you do not know what to say. You may be beautiful externally, but if you cannot answer the questions, you are likely not to make an impression of being beautiful on the inside. That means you won't be taken for the job. Appreciate what is on the inside of you. Celebrate your gifts, talents, the way you think, and the way you feel.

Your shape is beautiful, and your eyes are lovely; this will bring you favour in the midst of people. People will draw near to you when they behold your beauty, and they will be keen to know you. People will treat you well and value you highly. You are a very special individual, and your look is perfect.

When people see that you are beautiful and are also willing to go somewhere in life, they will support you. They will be amazed by your intelligence. They will even tell others about you and give a good reference *about* you. They will want to spend time with you.

You are beautiful and healthy, and that's great to know. Everybody knows that you are beautiful, but it is just that they haven't told you yet. Not everyone has the boldness to tell you that you are beautiful, so do not mind if you haven't been told. You might be wondering why you do not get compliments when you dress in your best. It is not that the people hate you or are jealous of your dressing; it is simply that they are shy to say their compliment, or they feel afraid to open their mouths. They do not know what you will think of them when they speak. They are scared of rejection.

Your close friends might tell you how good you look when you spend time with them. They might even appreciate you for how you carry yourself, your style of dressing, and your makeup. Always listen to great compliments and speak them into your life. Always keep an eye on people that tell you positive things about yourself, because they want the best for you.

Sometimes external beauty is not enough, if intelligence is not added to it. You are beautiful on the inside because of your intelligence, because you understand how you handle difficulties in life. Intelligence is your ability to stand out in the midst of difficulties. Your intelligence will make the world to appreciate you. Others will always remember you for it.

If you know that you are beautiful but do not feel that you are intelligent enough, I want you to know that you *are* intelligent. You are brilliant because your capability shows even in the smallest areas of your life. There is something that you know how to do, and you have done it well. You have tried. You have been able to overcome challenges, and you are still here today.

If you are beautiful and still wondering why people treat you badly, know that most people that behave like that have issues that they are going through in their own lives. When people have issues that they have not dealt with in their personal lives, they are hurting and are likely to throw it on others. They will not treat others right when they do not feel comfortable with themselves. Never feel that it is your fault when people do not treat you right. It has nothing to do with you. Say to yourself, 'I am not going to be concerned about this person. I am going to leave her to deal with her personal issues. I am moving on and have a bright future ahead of me. I have something big to achieve. I am too special to give up because of someone else's attitude or lack of intelligence.'

Whether you are skinny or fat, you still have to believe that you have a great figure that is amazing, and that people want to know you. You can't get yourself down by negative self-belief and the judgment of others. You are not a low person – you are high and beautiful. Your presence brings joy to the whole world. You are a good example and a source of greatness to others.

Sometimes I say to myself, 'I am as beautiful as Jerusalem.' Jerusalem is a very beautiful city. I say that I am as lovely as the city of Tirzah. I say to myself, ;I am the most beautiful of all women. I am different from everyone else, and there is something so wonderful about me.; Can you see that? I believe in myself even when I do not receive compliments from others. I know what I am, and I know I am made of good things.

You are beautiful and strong. You are one in ten thousand.

You have to believe in yourself no matter how you look. Your eyes are as beautiful as doves by a flowing brook. Your cheeks are as lovely as a garden that is full of herbs and spices. Your lips are like lilies, wet with liquid myrrh. Believe in yourself even if your friends do not believe in you.

Your hands are well formed, and your thighs are columns of alabaster set in sockets of gold. You are majestic like the Lebanon Mountains with their towering cedars. Your mouth is sweet to kiss, and everything about you is enchanting. You are beautiful, so start believing that today.

Your breath is like the fragrance of apples, your nose is as lovely as the tower of Lebanon, and your head is held high like the Mount Carmel. Your hair shines like the finest satin; its beauty would hold a king captive. You are amazing, and there is a lot for you to celebrate in yourself.

I want you to know that you are pretty. How pretty you are! How beautiful! You are as graceful as a palm tree. A palm tree is very tall and wide; that's why it is described as graceful. The grace you carry is great, and you are filled with love on the inside. You love people, and that is what makes you beautiful.

If you feel you aren't beautiful enough, you will still grow to be a beautiful person. It takes time to grow, and you must understand that. You are beautiful on the inside and outside, and that's the story; that's all you need to hear. Start believing in yourself now and showing how beautiful you are.

I know that you are strong and great. I know you are clothed with splendour. You are very special and have lots of beauty. You are not ordinary or here to be taken for granted. Your beauty is this great thing that everyone should know about. I feel like calling everyone to hear about you.

When people remember all the good things you have done, they will call you beautiful and will praise you for your work. You are not here for destruction or a waste of time. You are beautiful to behold, and that's the great news we all have to hear.

Your beauty, fame, powerful ruling, glory, and might will not end. You will not come down from your place of honour. You carry a beautiful crown, and no one is going to remove it from your head. You are crowned in the midst of what you are going through at the moment. You are blessed.

I want you to shine and appear excellently in the midst of your life difficulties and pain. You can shine just as you are.

You can show people that you are made of a beautiful glory and that nothing will stop you from making this known.

If you like wearing bracelets, wear them. Do whatever you like to make you look as beautiful as you want to be. Do not allow anyone to deceive you or tell you that it doesn't look good on you. As long as you have chosen it, then it should be right and suitable for you. As long as you believe in yourself, the world will believe in you.

However, do not overdo it, because too much of everything is not good. The main thing is to learn to satisfy yourself. As long as you are looking decent and modest, then that's great. Remember that your body is very important, and how you portray it to others tells them a lot about you.

You carry good news, and when people see, you they are excited about what they will hear. You are interesting and carry a great love for others. You know how to use your words in a positive manner. That's what I call self-celebration. You see, there is a lot for you to celebrate about yourself.

It is also a good thing to be beautiful and humble. In life it takes humility to operate under an authority. You need humility to receive correction and yet also do whatever you have been asked. When people see that you are beautiful and humble, they will draw near to you and wish to be like you. They will show their love towards you and be interested in you. They will want to learn more about who you are. They will want to give you help in different areas of your life.

Some people will want to correct you and let you know when you go wrong. They will also connect you to other opportunities when they see that you are humble. Humility helps you get along with people and treat them with value. The greatest of all is usually the servant of all. When you learn to serve people, they will give you a great seat.

However, adding humility to beauty does not mean you allow people to treat you like anyone. Do not allow others to look down at you or cast bad words at you. You have to remind them that you know your importance and appreciate yourself for who you are. They must know that you do not just give anything to yourself – you give the best.

If you feel that you are beautiful, but you feel crushed on the inside, then I want you to know that there is still time for you to rebuild yourself. There is still time for you to grow and get your balance right. You aren't going to feel crushed forever. You will come out of it with a smile on your face. You will turn up on the other side with a great smile. Your appearance carries dignity and beauty. If you do not know that, I want you to know it today. You have to start understanding who you are. Your good looks show that you respect yourself and that you can socialise easily with people of different groups. When you dress well, you feel free and have the boldness to communicate well.

If you feel you need some makeup to look beautiful, then put it on, but you must believe that the best lies inside of you. You are very great, and the world will turn to you with appreciation for your inner beauty. If you do not have the money to buy makeup, that doesn't mean the world has ended; you can still look your best by being simple but presenting yourself as a well-polished person.

You do not have to go for expensive things in order to look good. Some things are cheap but make you look decent, and you know that it is acceptable and still good. You don't have to believe in people out there wearing expensive things, because they do not believe in themselves. Give yourself the best that you can afford financially. Expensive things make no difference, especially when the inside is empty.

Your external appearance tells people how ready you are. If you are known by people for what you dress like, they will note it. They will see you as someone that is presentable and deserves to be taken somewhere. I believe you are ready to step into one of the best journeys of your life. Build a good presentation so that even if you meet a king on your way, you won't feel ashamed to go with him. Always be ready with your appearance.

Beauty brings perfection to things, and I am sure that when you see someone looking beautiful, your mind is filled with good memories. It is very interesting, and it's like good food for the eyes. Beauty is comely and acceptable, especially nowadays. There is nothing wrong with you looking beautiful. Beware of jealous people who are not happy to share in your joy because of your appearance.

Being mindful of your beauty means you are mindful of taking care of yourself. However, beauty is not everything; the world demands that we have other things outside beauty in certain circumstances. I have never seen anyone as ugly in my lifetime. What other people call ugliness is what I call uniqueness. My nose does not look like everyone's nose; it might look flat, but I like it the way it is. You have to believe that you are unique. We are all made up of different things. We all have different shapes of mouth, eyes, faces, and noses. I do not look like you, and you do not look like me. You should not say that you are more beautiful than me. We are all beautiful but in

Olly Sanya

different ways. I am talking about external beauty. In the end it is all beauty, and it makes the world more exciting.

We have to get to a level whereby we can celebrate the beauty of one another, because it is something great. Imagine seeing the same face all the time – you would be bored! When you see variety, then life becomes more interesting, and you can have something to think about and also celebrate.

You are beautiful in every way. You are beautiful on the inside and on the outside. You are beautiful amidst others and also when you are on your own. You are beautiful wherever you go. You are beautiful when you speak, and you are beautiful when you are quiet.

If you have a bad self-image, you will not be able to step out and do what you want to do. A bad self-image will prevent you from feeling like others, and in a place where others are doing great things, you will be unable to do something great. You do not have to hide your face from the crowd; know that you are capable, beautiful, and intelligent.

A bad self-image can make you fearful and shaky on the inside. You will lose your confidence if you do not possess a good self-image. You will not be able to settle down anywhere and will be moving from one place to the other.

You will not be able to confidently recognise who you are. That will not be your portion. You must have a good self-image that will help you to find your destiny.

A bad self-image will put you in bondage, whereby you will not feel free amidst others. I believe you do not want to feel caged up. You want your expectations to come true. You want your dreams to become a reality. You want to become one of the best. Therefore, get rid of that bad self-image. You are very wonderful and brilliant, so you do not possess a bad self-image. Grow into your greatness today and realise your worth.

As long as you have decided to put on a specific article of clothing, you should be proud about how you look in it. You should accept it and feel that it looks great on you. People love you out there and do not think your appearance is a hindrance. Shine with your appearance and put on your best, if you decide to do so. Do not allow anyone to stop you. Enjoy your day and have something to remember. Buy something expensive for yourself, if you choose to do so. You will see that as you desire to be your best, your days will glow, and you will be on top.

You are lovely in the eyes of others. You have done a lot of things for yourself, and people appreciate you for that. You are not rejected or alone; you are great in the midst of a group. You are very wonderful, and the good reputation you carry leaves a mark of beauty about you in the eyes of others. You are attractive and are able to attract the right partner into your life. Your appearance will click on the mind of the right partner when he or she sees you, and you will be joined together. You aren't going to remain single forever. One day that man or woman you are looking for will enter into your life. It will be easy, and you are going to celebrate yourself.

Your presence is eye-catching. When people see you, they are able to see beyond the normal eyes; they can see the greatness inside of you. They can see your wisdom, and they respect you for it. They know that you are of a great virtue and are going places in life. They know you for that, even if you do not know it yourself.

Do you believe you are a smart individual? You are definitely beautiful, but beyond that you are smart. You have lived for years in this world, and you have grown with intelligence. You have gained new skills and gained a new approach to dealing with your life problems. You speak with wisdom into the life of others, and they can see that inside of you.

Your presence is very appealing, and you are pleasant in the eyes of people. You attract people that are looking for good friendship. They seek people like you to encourage them in life. They want good people like you that can help them or show them the way; they want you to listen to them and be there for them. Therefore, celebrate yourself today because you are very pleasant, and people are pleased with you. You are worth a lot.

Your charisma also makes you beautiful. When you appear, you appear with joy and laughter, which makes the world more exciting for others. People are interested in you because of the way you carry yourself. You are very glad and full of joy, which makes you nice looking. You draw people to yourself like a magnet, and they do not want to leave you. They want to learn more about you. Your good mind towards others also makes you beautiful. You are willing to help and are ready to make other people's lives easier. You don't want them to go through more than they can bear. You are ready to convince them that there is more to life. A good mind entices others to be with you because they know you want good for them.

Your personality has spread good news about you, and even people that you do not know respect you for being yourself. They say to themselves, 'What an exciting person.' They see that you know how to deal with people and are a good person on the inside. They know that you do not create trouble; instead, you live a peaceful life.

You have a good sense of yourself, and even though you are not perfect, you know you are trying your best every day. You are ready to make an effort and have a clue of what you are like; you know you aren't a bad person. You have seen people make good comments about you, and you have seen yourself repeat your good deeds again and again. Well done for that! You are doing brilliantly.

In life, never think wrong of yourself no matter the mistakes you make. Never judge yourself wrongly. Always protect your self-image by speaking positive words into your life. Remember the good things you do and celebrate yourself for them. Don't see yourself as someone that doesn't know how to do anything right. View yourself as a very capable person who is able to be an example to others. Appreciate your good sides and make a great celebration about it. Always honour yourself every time you act in a good way towards someone else or yourself. Always keep a good record of your rights and ignore your wrongs. Lift yourself up; don't throw yourself down. Always know you are worth much more.

**The lessons you learn today bring out your best.
Your best is guaranteed to bring self-celebration.**

Chapter 15
You Have Learnt

You have learnt a lot of lessons in your life that have built you up for excellence. The lessons you have learnt make you a mature person and a better you. Do not allow people to interfere with your personal life. Life is very personal, and we have all learnt different lessons. You do not go through what your friend is going through; what you are going through is different. Stand strong and always apply the personal lessons you have learnt in your life to the things you do. Do not let anyone stop you.

The lessons you learn in life are what carry you and help you build a life of full success and greatness. When you make a mistake, it looks like you have fallen, but it's really the beginning of your rising. You are only going to rise higher and become great.

You do not have to remember the pain behind the lessons you have learnt. You simply have to enjoy where you are today and remember your past with a smile. You don't have to look at the things that haven't worked out. You should be glad that the lessons you have learnt have brought you this far.

You have learnt to love people despite their bad sides. You love the world, and you love to help people. The same love you show will return to you. People do appreciate you for your love; you are valued by your family and close friends. You have done a lot for people, and they do appreciate it. Love is the greatest gift. The love you have shown is like a sacrifice which was not easy. Well done.

The lessons you have learnt in life are going to bring you great rewards in the future. You can only climb higher in life because there is no way down. You are going to live each day in a successful way. You are going to be capable to the extent that you will be able to achieve the impossible. The lessons you have learnt in life will help you to celebrate yourself. They will make you produce a better piece of work in every area of your life. You will wake up and realise the facts of life. The lessons you have learnt will make you understand the standard of life and keep you working towards it. You will produce things of higher quality because you have learnt from your mistakes of yesterday.

Sometimes a person walks into your life and teaches you a lesson. The person did not walk into your life by mistake; it was meant to be. You notice that after the person leaves you, you become more perfect and sharper in dealing with similar experiences in the future. You become more brilliant anytime you go through an experience. It shows people how good you are and helps you shine more. People that walked into your life have exposed you to what you want to become. You have grown up to become a more mature individual due to that experience. People help you figure out who you are. You have discovered new capabilities that are inside of you through the difficult time you've had with people. You have seen that you are actually stronger than you thought. They have built you up and made you more attentive to how you should live your life. They have shaped you into a more focused and strengthened person.

Others do affect your life no matter how small the time they spend with you. People are very powerful, and their presence is very strong. You can't get rid of them, but they have influenced you to become a better person. They make you have more concern for your future when they mistreat you. They have taught you to love yourself more and to focus on making yourself a better person. They teach you different lessons and help you realise your strength. You learn that you can do something better or function in a more capable manner after someone comes into your life and shakes you up. They helped you understand yourself better and discover new talents that are inside of you. When you mix with people, your life can never be the same; their presence will always make a difference. The tough time they tend to give you will turn you into a more powerful person and bring success to your life.

People help you realise your willpower. The lessons you have learnt about people make you more determined in life. The way they correct you has made you to think about how you can become sharper. You have improved because of the time you spent with them. You can resolve issues in a better way now after people have walked into your life. They helped you built a stronger spirit and made you more motivated.

Some people who have walked into your life in the past have led to your successes or downfalls. You have learnt to be more careful with people and not simply commit yourself to individuals without trying to get to know them first. You now know how to pick the right people for your destiny. You don't just go for anything people say, like you did before; you listen more carefully before you make your decisions.

People have built the strength of your character; they

have helped you behave better and carry yourself with more dignity. Even though it is painful when people let you down or look down or you, it only makes you a stronger person. The next time, you will dress better and speak better because you do not want that shameful act of others towards you to repeat itself.

The things you do to yourself and the ways you treat yourself are better than before. You have learnt not to give everything to others while leaving yourself empty. You have learnt to focus more on yourself and build a great life for yourself. You have learnt to desire better things for yourself in the midst of others. You have learnt to use your talents more and respect yourself. You are more cautious in life and you do not just do things on a whim. You know how to take care of the things you have. You are more protective and do not expose what you have to just anybody. You are more alert and watch over the things you have in a better way than before. You can observe people very well now compared to before. You observe their behaviour from a distance and can tell what to expect from them, whether good or bad.

You are more current and on the lookout for what goes on in the world. You can learn from the mistakes that others have made; you do not want to fall into the same trap that someone else fell into yesterday. You can pay attention to how others are living their lives, and you are attentive to the things that benefit them. Then, you can apply the good principles to your own life.

A person like you, who has learnt a lot of lessons in life, deserves to celebrate. What else are you looking for? Whom are you waiting for in order to celebrate yourself? The fact that you have come a long way means you need to celebrate yourself. I want you to have that special joy of self-celebration. You have dealt with things well, and now you need to celebrate yourself, knowing that you are indeed someone.

You have studied yourself better and know the things that work for you. You know what is good for you and what is bad for you. You know what your body and spirit likes, and you know how to protect yourself from the things that you do not like. You know the sort of people that bring favour to your life, as well as the ones that do not. That's part of the lessons you have learnt for yourself. You know how to live a life that will bring you happiness and great blessings for your benefit.

You have adjusted yourself and have seen the difference between where you were yesterday and where you are today. You have gained new skills and learnt new things.

You have been exposed to different experiences and have tapped into the things that you feel will benefit you. You have corrected your ways and have come out to be a more pleasant person. Well done.

You have learnt to open your eyes to little things, which do matter. There was a time that I forgot to check the bin in my house. I thought it was okay because I always cleaned it, and it looked perfect. The bin had a leak, though, and a little child that came into the house poured a drink into the bin; the liquid messed up the whole carpet in the room. At that point, I learnt to start looking out at the little things.

You have learnt to talk to people that you haven't talked to before. Before you ignore people, especially new faces, take the time to hold a short conversation with them. It might be the person that will help you to become a bigger person in life. People come in disguise sometimes, and the ones that you think do not matter are often the ones that turn out to be the best out of the group.

Learn to hold your head up even when things don't work out. The former project you were working on did not look successful in the beginning, but later on it turned out to be a great one, bringing you favour and goodness. Never give up. Continue and persevere even when it seems the sky is not a clear blue; you can still hope for the colour blue to reappear.

You are not in the place you were before, because you have learnt to always move forward. No matter how tough things are, there is still a lot you can do with your life. Enjoy life and create pleasure for yourself. You have learnt that life has a lot in store for you, and you have discovered that there are greater things inside of you. The best thing about your mistake is that it doesn't break you – it only builds you. It opens a wider door in front of your eyes with great choices. Your mistakes do not have to make you sorrowful; they can make you sharper and build your talents and abilities. Your mistakes make you more intelligent and well defined. You won't remain the same person; instead, mistakes makes you look more talented and extraordinary in the eyes of others. You are very great.

If you can dream it, you can do it. Dreams are not a joke and do become realities with time. Dreams take you into a process machine that builds you up for the harvest time. You have probably dreamed about something and then saw that thing happen. Therefore you do not have to be afraid or feel down when it seems that your dreams do not happen in the time you expect. As long as it is inside of you, it will happen one day. You become what you think about.

Keep thinking those good things about yourself; keep your mind focused on what's beautiful. Keep thinking that you are in charge and are a leader. You will grow to become what you are thinking of in time.

Don't judge each day by the harvest you reap but by the seeds you sew. Not reaping what you have sowed do not mean it's the end of life. When you do anything good, you sow a seed, but the result of that goodness does not have to come on the same day you did the good thing; it may come later on, but the important thing is that you have done something powerful for the day, and that lies in your seed. No seed is going to go wasted; it will all count in the future.

Even when you do not get the result you are expecting, you can still celebrate the fact that you are doing a great job. You are doing your part right, and that's what you have to celebrate. The answer is not necessary no when you do not get the result immediately. The fact that you found out that things did not work out as you planned doesn't mean you haven't done well. You are really trying, and the universe appreciates that.

Not achieving the right outcome today doesn't mean you won't have the chance to achieve it in the future. The thing you produced might not look perfect today, but I want you to know that tomorrow you will do something excellent and will see a great result.

You will learn in life that you are better off spending your time thinking and planning instead of worrying. You don't have to fret about the things that are not working right in your life; you don't have to be troubled because you did not get what you wanted. Don't be too concerned about the things that have not yet come your way. Instead, think of great ideas and plan ahead; prepare for the next opportunity that is coming your way, and make a great proposal of what you want to achieve next. Let your advanced worrying be replaced by advanced planning.

If you have the courage to begin, you have the courage to succeed. The fact that you are able to start something with boldness means you can get to the place of your success. It might not come now, but it will still come. Always be keen to start things, especially without being told by others. Your desire to do something that really matters will bring you success in life. You have to activate the dreams in you by starting in one place, and then you can grow to become bigger and better.

The lessons you have learnt make you sharper. You become a pillar of fire to enemies when you learn from your mistakes in life. You become a piercing sword to the things

193

that can hinder your bright future. The lessons of life build you up to become quicker at attacking what hinders you. You become a greater individual as you learn daily in life, and you shine more.

The lessons you have learnt make you stronger. I know you are strong, but when you learn from your mistakes, you become stronger. You are able to defend yourself more and choose the finer things in life for yourself. You are able to become more fervent after you have gone through hard times. You go deeper into aspects of your life and build something stronger for yourself. The lessons you have learnt help you build your future. You will be able to shake off any obstacles. You will become well constructed on the inside as you go through the lessons you learn each day. You will be able to put yourself together in a powerful way, forming something greater for yourself that will count towards your future.

It doesn't matter if you are a slow walker, as long as you don't walk backwards. You might be doing something slowly, but I tell you, the slow ones are usually the greatest. They end up on top compared to those that are fast. You being slow in doing something does not mean you are sluggish; you are still the best of your kind, and I want you to know that if you are facing forward, you are going somewhere in life.

Part 3

Actions That Can Hinder Self-Celebration

There is no point in sharing the good things about your life with the wrong person. Don't feel bad if others do not approve of your self-celebration.

Chapter 16
Telling the Wrong Person

Not everyone will be happy with your self-celebration. Not everyone is willing to celebrate you. You are better off keeping away from people that do not show interest in you practising the principles of self-celebration. You don't have to go along with people that are not ready to celebrate you. Not every good that happens in your life should be shared. You have to be careful about what you say. Some people are very wicked, to the extent that if they know your source of joy, they will try to stop it. They are not happy themselves and are not interested in your happiness.

However, I am sure you have a few people in your life that are glad about your celebration. You should keep close to people like that and be there for them. You should build good relationship with good people. You have to be smart and focused on the people that make you relax, feel confident, and laugh. Stay with people who make you happy.

Sometimes you can exchange phone numbers, especially when you meet people that are keen towards you. Find people that watch out for your well-being and are willing to protect you from the wickedness of this world. It's not everywhere you go in life that you will find people that are ready to leave themselves and focus on you. However, if you find such a person, be grateful about it.

Life is very selfish, and people are more concerned about themselves, focusing on how they will make it in life. Instead of helping others, they want others to be down so that they have a reason to laugh. There are people with evil, hidden agendas that are not willing to hear that you are celebrating yourself.

You can easily read the motives of others. The question is, how do you know if this is a wrong person? Listen to what people say and check whether they still maintain their smile when they hear that you are celebrating yourself. You do not have to tell the wrong people about your self-celebration because they will intentionally discourage you and make you feel like you do not deserve to be celebrated. They will tell you things that you do not want to hear, such as, 'You are not a winner.' You need to stay around people who will speak words of love into your life, who will not wrong you, who are always happy to see you and are keen to protect your name behind your back.

People have different ways in which they think, and even if you tell them that you are celebrating yourself, they might not understand. You are the only one that can understand why you are celebrating yourself. They might not see the reason for celebration. Sometimes if people do not know you very well, they can mistreat you and not celebrate with you. Use your talents in their presence, and they will understand you. People that remind you about your past are not the best to tell about your self-celebration. Even though they have seen you excel in their presence, they are still wicked and stubborn.

Some people remind you of your weaker days. These sorts of people are not the ones that you should tell about your self-celebration. They find a reason to claim that they are better than you. They always give you a bad look, and they tell you that you are worth nothing. The wrong people are the ones that go behind your back to gossip about you and search for faults within your excellence. Avoid people that bring you discomfort through their actions or words; they will leave you with pain and make your mind linger on bad things.

Some people lack good counsel and do not have people in their lives that speak good things to them. Therefore they are not happy and content about their lives. These kinds of people will not be keen to celebrate you. Do not stay around people that reject you; they do not believe in your dreams and do not want you to get the best in life. These kinds of people can spoil your day, and you are better off keeping away from them. Every individual has a way of operating in life. Some people meet you for the first time and keep their impression of you; even if you change in the future, they will not believe in you. Such people do not deserve your presence.

People are raised up in different families and have been taught different things. They have been mistreated in different ways. You cannot expect others to get rid of what they have been taught, which forms part of how they view things in life. Some people have been injured on the way to their destinies; they do not have people that they can always look to in times of need. People like that are likely not to be interested in your self-celebration. They do not celebrate others due to their own insecurities. They like to rule and feel on top, and they do not like to give other people chances. People like that are not likely to be interested in your self-celebration. They do not know how to do anything right because they have been told that they cannot make it or become better in life. People like that will not give you a chance to celebrate yourself in their presence.

Some people have been under bad leaders in different areas of their lives, and those leaders did not remind them to add value to their lives. They do not understand what value is, and they are likely to lack self-respect. Anyone that lacks self-respect can never respect or celebrate others.

Speak to the right people that will encourage you and lift you up. You need people in your life that will help build your confidence by celebrating with you. People that will cheer you up are the ones to whom you should go. You need people who will promote the goodness in your life, who want you to get better.

Speak to those that understand you. People that understand you are able to persuade you regarding what you are thinking of going for. They will motivate you, lead you rightly, and be happy for you. You need people that appreciate your success and think of you even when you aren't around. Speak to those that know you well and understand from where you are coming. Find people that have seen you when you laboured and appreciate the efforts you have made. You need people that are able to recognise you with your talents; they have seen you performed and love what you do. You need people that realize who you are and know your good deeds.

Keep far away from people that easily discourage you. You need to feel lifted in life, and there is nothing wrong with feeling happy. You should always shine with your joy and be delighted about yourself. You should feel a great deal of pleasure in knowing yourself for who you are. You deserve to be thrilled about your current performance and lifestyle.

You need people in your life that can be part of your self-celebration. These people should communicate well to others about you and spread the news about your great performances. You need people that can feel pleasant about you celebrating yourself and share your feelings of happiness. They can listen to you share what is making you happy, sense your positive emotions, and in turn say 'Well done' to you.

Speak to those with whom you can share your good moods. When you feel very happy about yourself and believe you have achieved something that means a lot to you in a day, you should have people in your life that you can talk to about it. They are the people that will continually motivate you and help you see yourself as the best.

Speak to people that have a high opinion of you. Those

who respect you are the ones with whom you should share your celebration. They view you as someone that is worthy and deserving of great things. They honour you and hold you with respect. They speak good things about you and are waiting to see you shine in your tomorrow.

Speak to people who believe in you and your dreams, and who know that you are very capable. They should be ready to celebrate your life and be happy about where you are going. People that do not change their minds about you, even when you make a mistake, are the ones you need in your life.

Do not tell the wrong type of person, because that person will not be impressed by what you want to share. You need the right person, who will consider what you are saying and be able to agree with you. The right person will be filled with joy when he hears what you are talking about. The right person will make you feel happier and more determined about your future.

The wrong person will not be affected by what you say. Instead of listening to you, he might say he doesn't have time, or he calls you proud. Celebrating yourself has nothing to do with pride; it is a practical and normal thing. Only those who understand it will create room for it.

The right person will understand how you feel and will share in your joy. She will celebrate you and rejoice with you. The right person won't treat you like a small person; she will treat you like a wonderful person. The right person will express her joy towards what you have achieved in life and will make you feel very proud of yourself. She will be pleased with you when you share things about your self-celebration. She will be cheered up because of the good news that you have to share. The person will celebrate the quality of your life with you and will see you as someone in the forefront. You will feel very superior.

The right person will make you feel like an excellent person. You should feel proud of the hard work you have done in your life when you speak to the right person. You will feel like you have done something outstanding in your life. You will feel like you are exceptional and have raised the standard in your performance. You can be on top and admired by others. You will think of yourself as a superb person.

The right person will join you in the place you are being celebrated, and that person will tell others about how good you are. She will lift your name high and elevate you beyond the normal, building your name for others and will make sure you are seen as a top person. The right person will make you feel very good about yourself. She will make others see you as a great person and will exalt you during your celebration time.

The right person will make you a point of contact for others. She will help others connect with you and find a reason to always be with you. The person will make you very happy, like you are the best in the world. The words of the right person will help you forget about the bad things that have happened in your past; you will think better of yourself. She will possess a very good character which you like and which puts a smile on your face. The person will possess a good nature that will soothe you, and her words will be a source of healing to your soul. The person's personality will be something that you will see as a blessing and a source of joy.

Search for like-minded individuals who share similar interests with you. People that have the same things that you have will feel comfortable on your level and will be willing to open up to you and listen to you. They will be a great sort of support to you and will understand what it feels like to walk in your shoes.

If you spot an individual that shows respect to you, try to connect with the person. If you meet people that talk to you in a good way and respect your personality, connect with them. Remember that your nature is very important, and you have to protect your mind. Good people will always promote you for who you are.

Search for the right people when you have the opportunity to be in new groups. You can never tell how wonderful the people near you can be unless you talk to them. Open up to new faces and share small talk. Investigate the characters of people you meet on your journey and select the right people that can support your destiny and self-celebration. Remember that you have a beautiful future ahead of you, so, never give up. Keep going because you will achieve greater things than you expected.

Forget about previous bad events so that you can be happy and celebrate yourself.

Chapter 17
Remembering Your Past

If you remember your past in a negative way, then you cannot celebrate yourself. You have to let go of your past and not dwell in it. I understand we all have a past, and it's not easy to let go of its events. However, you can still get up and say to yourself, 'I am going to forget about this; I'm about to move on.' Leave the past where it is and reach for the future. The past is not going to do anything for you, but you can prepare for the future. Make the future brighter and sweeter. You might not believe me, but you have the power to do so. You can say to yourself, 'My future is going to be one of the best, and I am going to come out tall.'

Your life wants to produce more. You have many victories today compared to yesterday. Your tomorrow also contains more blessings than today. The impact you will make in the world is big, and people are waiting for you. Your presence is special, and there is a lot for you to catch. You have not done your best yet – your best improves every day. If you are a teacher, you have not yet taught your best lessons. Get your hope up and prepare for greater things. There is no limit to your greatness, and the earth has the space for you to be all you want to be.

I want you to see yourself as a very great person who is unbeatable and will be moving forward. You have a lot to achieve ahead of you, and you are going to fly in the future. You are going to do things that you have not done before. There is something brighter waiting ahead of you. Leave the past behind and march into the future. Do not have low expectations – expect something high, and you will receive it! Make great plans for yourself and do not settle for anything less. Don't compare your talent to others. The talent you have is very special.

Get rid of the defeated mindset that make you think little of yourself and that tell you that you can't do anything better. Be careful of those mindsets. You are a very special person and were made to be a champion. You have a great life that is supernatural and filled with quality treasures. Such is the type of life that you will live. You are going to come out as a winner. You have everything it takes to make it. The seed of success is inside of you – you just have to tap into it. You have the ability to continuously repeat the actions that create a fully maximised life. Do not let anyone tell you that you lack wisdom, determination, or creativity. The ideas of success are inside you.

You know what to do; you aren't a fool. You can be determined and can apply the wisdom needed. You are an individual created for success. Sit down and enjoy what life has to offer you.

The events of your past do not reduce your potential. You have to take a step of faith, and then you'll rise higher. Your life history may look funny, but that does not mean that you cannot step into a bigger future. It doesn't stop you. The mistakes you have made earlier in your life do not limit where you are going. The previous acts you took which doesn't seem right has no power to stop you from stepping into the future. You are done with your past. The mistakes you have made are over. You are greater than your mistakes. You are more than your fall. You are going to step above the mistakes because you can only go higher. Your position is above, and you are going to shine like you never have before. You are larger than any mistake that you can ever make on the surface of this earth.

You are better than the mistakes you made yesterday. You are a superior being and can use your mistakes to your advantage. You are huge in your own way. In the future, you will be a famous person and will realise the fact that your mistake is only a source of favour. You have improved more compared to the mistakes you have made in your past. The experiences which you do not like have made you into a healthier person today. Your past helps you beat your enemies, showing you how strong you are and how better you can be. It reveals your new strengths and prepares you to outshine your peers. The past enhances your skills and abilities and makes you perform your best. It has taught you to always be on top, and in anything you do nowadays, you seem to be better than others. You have seen yourself move to a higher place in life due to the mistakes you have made in your past. You have been able to recover from your little places, and now you are on top. If you aren't there yet, you will get there.

You can use your gifts and talents in a better way. Maybe there are areas in your life where you haven't used your talents. Start using them now, and you will be recognised. You should always learn to try again despite your failures. Maybe you've asked for something a thousand times, and you haven't received it yet. Ask again. You have to push – you can't stop.

Your gifts and talents have the power to wipe away your past. Your gifts and talents are the present that you have for the world. It is this special thing inside of you for which others will lift you up. It will make others proud of you. Your gifts and talents represent your contribution in making this world a better and more suitable place for everyone. Your gifts and talents bring you a great sense of satisfaction.

You can lose energy, passion, and direction by only remembering your past. You do not want to feel drained; you want to feel energised. You want to feel encouraged, so why do you keep dwelling on the past? You have to move higher and enjoy your life to the fullest. You have to do the things that you have decided to do. There is a lot ahead of you. You need a life that is full of greatness and inspiration. You can remember the good things in your past and celebrate them. The bad things of your past have to leave you. The past can be very difficult to let go of, but you have to try. You will feel degraded when you remember your negative past. Remembering the past can steal your motivation and make you feel that you cannot make it. That's not your destiny, so march forward.

You want a life that is full of motivation and that will stimulate you to go beyond normal and do things that are great. Your life should be a source of encouragement to you, not a source of destruction. Therefore you need to remove any bad ideas that you have in your mind regarding yourself. Discard those negative things that you think about and make you feel down.

You have to keep your thoughts clean towards yourself, so don't allow the negative past to remove the quality way you view yourself. You have to keep seeing yourself as an excellent person. See yourself as someone that has a great character. You should always lift yourself up high in life, valuing what is inside of you. Keep the good things that are inside of you and see yourself as a superior person. You are not inferior.

Why should you allow your past to make you think less of yourself? I challenge you to think of yourself in a better manner. You don't have to believe that you are a little person who does not have what it takes to achieve great heights. You don't have to keep reflecting on the evil events that happened to you in your past; by reflecting on them, you will feel discouraged. You have to start imagining yourself in a great way. Imagine yourself stepping into a greater position. Think of something big about yourself; see yourself ruling and climbing up in life. Visualise yourself taking charge and controlling things as a champion who deserves to win over any obstacles. Whatever you see is going to happen to you.

Maybe, there are people whose actions gave you a bad

past. Leave those people alone, because you cannot change them. If you've worked hard as a parent, but your children have not produced good results in the past, you simply have to hope for the future. They will still get better, and something good will still come out of them. You have to keep believing.

The past can put a lot of pressure on you: it can blame you for not being a perfectionist. You have to let all the blame go and regain yourself. You have to believe in the precious you and know that you can make something better out of your tomorrow. You have to keep going, knowing that your best is yet to come. Your past does not have to control you in anyway. You have to plan ahead and use your today to delete your past. You must know that you have tried to be your best, and anyone that's not happy with it can go away. They don't have to be happy – *you* have to be happy with yourself. People don't have to be satisfied through you; they can get their satisfaction elsewhere.

Your bad past does not have the power to manage your present. It doesn't have the power to organise how things are going to go for you, and it has no say in your future because it cannot limit where you can go. Your past cannot rule over your present or stop your happiness. Your bad past cannot manipulate you or influence you negatively.

It can't direct you to the wrong places or steal what is important in your life. You have to go for the best – don't let your past create the belief in your heart that you cannot make it. Do not allow the past of your partner to affect you. You might be doing your part in a relationship, but the other person is not giving much in return. You have to focus on what you have done right and hope that the other person will change. You don't have to allow the other person to make you sad or control you. You should live your own life and enjoy the things in store for you.

You do not have to feel depressed, thinking you've let others down. Even those you feel you've let down still appreciate and recognise you. You are human, and humans are not perfect. You do not have to carry the loads of others. The fact that you helped them does not mean you are responsible for their entire lives.

If others complain about your past, it does not mean anything. You cannot make them be like you; you cannot make them feel grateful. If they do not appreciate what you have done for them in the past, then stop helping them. Let them go fend for themselves. They are capable of sorting out their own problems. You can step back in the area of helping everybody. You do not have to satisfy anyone else. If you have done what your power can afford, and you can't do anything further, then leave it there. You cannot make everybody happy. Focus on your own happiness and self-celebration.

Maybe you are operating out of guilt, and you are doing things because people say you have not tried enough. You do not have to over-commit yourself to people because you want to please them. You may feel that you will hurt their feelings if you do not go an extra mile, but take it easy and remember that you are not responsible for making their lives work right.

Sometimes it is good when an opportunity comes to an end. The next opportunity might be an even greater one! Life has a lot of chances for you. When you get one wrong, another chance will come. It is never too late for you to make it. Always think of the good things and wish yourself well in life. Your successes, victories, and good times are what you should always remember and hope for.

Sometimes you have to stop and celebrate yourself. You should remember the good things you have done. It is not an optional thing to celebrate you – it's compulsory. You have to celebrate the positive influence you have made in the community, in your family, and in your groups. You have to celebrate the quality of life you are living. You have to celebrate the respect you have for yourself.

You have to celebrate the upright life you are living. You should celebrate the fact that you are worthy to be praised for the things that you have done. You have to celebrate the blameless life you have lived. You ought to celebrate the fact that you have not been a source of problem to anybody. You have kept your path right and clean, minding your own business.

If you have some memorial stories about the good things you have experienced, they will encourage you and keep you going. Remember when a door opened for you where it looked like there was no door? Remember when you got that job in the midst of your financial difficulties? You should be grateful for instances like that and celebrate them.

Remember how you overcame a life storm? Be grateful about it. If you are aware of life's goodness on the inside, then you won't go around thinking like a failure. You will say to yourself, 'if I can experience this goodness of life once, it will happen to me again.' You have to think about the good things on purpose and celebrate the good events that happened in your life. Maybe you used to think negatively before, but today you are a positive person, and that's something to be grateful about. Maybe you've suffered from all kinds of addictions and bad habits, but today you've come out of it, and that's something to be grateful for. Celebrate these things!

You can remove your past by celebrating your today. When you start celebrating the good achievements you have made possible today, you will smile. You will not have negative thoughts on your mind regarding your past. You will be happy to look back, and you will always have reasons to be grateful and joyful at heart, until you achieve all your goals.

Do not speak bad things into your life; they will build negative thoughts and will prevent you from saying, 'I want to celebrate myself.'

Chapter 18
Negative Self-Prophecies

I know that you are used to the way you live your life. You have a way in which you do things, and you might be comforted by it. However, this is a time for change. You might not understand what negative self-prophecies are. Negative self-prophecies are the wrong and negative things you say to yourself. You should not continue to speak negative things to yourself. Words that are imperfect do not soothe you.

You are greater than you think you are. You don't have to say things that are unenthusiastic to yourself. Things like that can make you feel down and can even affect your health. Remember that you are a very special individual, and that there is nothing that the world can do to you to make you give up. You have to hold up to who you are and remain focused on the fact that you have a bright future. There are brighter days ahead of you; you are going to shine.

You do not have to lose that special interest that you have in yourself. I want you to start believing in yourself like you did before. Keep that happiness and joy that flows on the inside anytime you remember yourself. Keep allowing that beauty of grace that you carry to shine, even in the eyes of others. Do not lose your hope. Keep going – you are going to make it!

Please do not belittle yourself down in life. Allow that light that you carry to shine brighter. Keep working hard and moving on with your life. Retain that pride that you have towards yourself, and do not allow anyone to discourage you. You have a lot to offer in this world, and people are waiting for you to rise. You will be exalted.

Negative self-prophecies can make you lose your joy, focus, happiness, and drive. Instead of speaking negative self-prophecies, you can decide to speak powerful and positive words into your life. You have to keep saying those positive words. I know you might be thinking, 'I am tired of speaking those words. They do not happen!' It's going to happen one day: those problems are going to be fixed, and you will enjoy the best of your life.

Your life will be built on a strong foundation when you speak positive words into your life. You will not just be ordinary – you will extraordinary. You will be on top and far above others. You will win and will overcome your challenges. You will not live a simple and sluggish life when you speak positive words into your life; instead, you will be a champion and a forerunner who is fast in producing great results. You will run your race swiftly and will end up great.

Please do not tell people negative things about yourself, because it will not help. Do you know you are a great individual? You are not a small person – you were made for a purpose. People like to hear things, and sometimes you like to tell them about your life. There is nothing wrong with that, but there is something wrong with you saying things that are not good all the time. You have to rise and discover who you are. You have to see that the best lies inside of you. You should make others proud of you by telling them great and exciting things about your life so that they will view you positively. You should never speak negative into your life. Your words are going to come true one day. Others will think of you as a great individual; they will believe in you and will want to be with you. They will like you and even wish to be like you. They will learn from you and will want your presence to have an impact on their lives.

Nowadays, there are a lot of wicked people that cannot wait to hear you speak badly of yourself, because they will use it against you. Try not to mingle with people like that. Mix with those who love you and say good things about you. Keep yourself apart from anyone who wants you to be down and from those who do not want you to believe in yourself. Walk with those that are keen towards you when you are celebrating yourself.

Whatever you say about yourself will become a reality one day. The things you say will not waste away – they will surely happen. Your words carry power and shape your life. You might not understand it, but I will help you understand it. Your words flow towards your future, shaping your thinking and affecting how you carry yourself. If you speak powerful words into your life, you will carry yourself in a great and special way. On the other hand, if you speak negative words into your life, you will be sluggish and unproductive.

I understand we all get tired of a present situation and just want to say it as it is. You may say that to someone who is very close to you, or to anyone who can provide a solution or words of comfort. There is no reason to say it to people who are not ready to provide solutions. Share your secrets with a close and understanding person who will in turn speak positive and powerful words into your life.

You are not an average person; you might be average today,

but in your future you will be great. Speak things of the future into your life. Prepare for your future by speaking positive words into your life. Maybe you are saying, 'Others are better than me.' I want you to know that you are better than others, and as you take a step, your life will not be the same. Your life is going to change, and you will win lots of medals. You will go out with boldness and fulfil your purpose. You will be outstanding in your future. You will be called for honour, you will be influential, you will be magnificent, you will be very strong, and you will be significant. Great people will be your friends, and you will walk with kings and queens. You will be lifted, you will be treated specially, you will be a star, and your light will be very bright.

Negative words build low self-esteem. When you hear negative words about your life, you are likely to feel down. You cannot feel confident through negative words, which eat you up and leave you feeling crushed. They can also lead to self-destruction. Do not keep saying negative things about yourself. Speak words that will guide you into the future and will lift you up, turning your life around for the better.

You do not want to develop into someone that is going nowhere in life. That's what negative words do. Rise today and realise who you are. Discover the precious seeds of magnificence inside you. It's high time you see that you are too great for that mess. You might not have people that are speaking great words into your life but, that doesn't mean you can't do it for yourself. You can start now and know that you will be on the road to success.

You will have great achievements in this life through your positive self-prophecies. You will accomplish things that are beyond the natural, and you will rise into greater levels in every aspect of your life. Remember that your words are powerful and can lead to your victory or failure. Speak great words into your life so that they can prepare you for the greatest of your days. You will triumph in every area of your life. You are going to hit the high places in life. You are going to beat your enemies through the achievements of your tomorrow. You are going to smack down those little defeats. You are going to come out as a winner and on top. You are going to reach a place in your life where you will feel very secure about your achievements; all your fears will be gone. You are going to arrive at a great destination that will soothe you.

Another reason why we say negative self-prophecies is because we do not feel we have what it takes to achieve a purpose. My dear, there is a lot on the inside of you. You might feel that you do not have what it takes to achieve something, but all you need is to try. When you try, you take a step for a greater future. You have good skills and abilities – even smiling at someone is a skill. I know you have what it takes to become whatever you want to become in life, and you will get there.

You need to learn to speak great words into your life, such as, 'I am very capable. I can make it. I am an over comer. I am different. I will surely be a success.' Speak those words into your life; write them down and remind yourself about them every day. Keep saying them until you overcome those obstacles and get to your desired destination. Your words are not going to fail; they will make sense one day, and you will grow into a mighty person.

Speak words that will edify you. Words that edify you will bring comfort into your life and change how you view the world. The way you view your negative experiences will be different when you start speaking great words into your life. You will see in a different way. You will visualize yourself climbing higher and achieving the impossible.

Speak words that will enlighten you about your future and that will motivate you to do what you have not done before. You need words that will carry you through your present storm and place you on a rock. On the rock, you will stand firm, and no river will be able to move you. Those words will guide you and lead you to success, protecting your life through tough times.

Positive words can create a positive atmosphere. If you are going through a bad situation at the moment, learn to speak positive words into your life. Do not mind who is around you – say it out. You can also record it and play it again and again. Those positive words will produce a good impression in your spirit and will make you feel very happy. They will change your mood from a bad one to a good one.

You might be in a bad environment at the moment; maybe it's because you do not have the money to afford your own accommodations. If you speak positive words, the environment will change into a positive and lively one. The surroundings will become more suitable and satisfying for you, and you can manage until you get to move on. You have the power to change the difficult things through words.

Great words can make you to create great plans for your life. Bad words torment you, but positive words are likely to motivate you and help you see yourself as greater than your situations. You can say to yourself every day, 'I am a winner,' and you will become one. Before you know it, you will have the mindset of a winner. You will begin to think well of yourself and see yourself as a more capable person. You will overcome your lows, and you will get high.

Great words can erase your bad past. The good words you speak into your life today will make you to forget the hurt and pain. They will give you joy, and you will no longer worry about the past. You will be filled with victory and a sense of a bright future compared to the past. You will be a winner in the forefront, and you will get things done. You will be moving on to become the best for yourself, and you will no longer remember your challenges.

Great words can give you a positive attitude and the bravery to try new things that may be beyond your capability. Then you will start thinking higher and planning for new things to happen to you. You will be very focused and you will be looking forward to the brighter tomorrow. Great words that you speak to yourself can make you approach anything in life; you will be able to face any situation, and what people see as difficult, you will see as easy. Great words can give you a positive outlook to life, and you will be able to thrive anywhere.

Positive words can give you a good day, no matter how bad your day is. The great words you speak into your life will be like a defence against the bad things you experience. Your words will be like a ladder that enables you to climb over those difficulties. You will go through the day with positive thoughts and feelings of great happiness, instead of being sad and down.

Great words will give you a great mindset that will enable you to think through problems and see them as nothing. You will be greater than the challenges that come your way. You will be very intelligent in your response to problems, and you will be very sharp in the words you issue to deal with them. You will be able to use your smart mentality to conquer problems even before they start. You will be ahead of problems, and no fire will touch you at all.

Great words can renew your mind. When you speak great words into your life, the bad things you are thinking of will disappear; your mind will be clear and sound. You will be filled with energy and a great strength towards the future. Your mind will be clean. I want you to know that there is a high possibility for success ahead of you, and there is a door that will be opened before you. You will experience wonders.

Positive words can make you a champion. You can win over whatever you are going through when you speak great words into your life; you will come out stronger, and you will be able to maintain your smile regardless of how difficult the situation is.

Great words can influence you positively and give you the power to go for what you want. They will set you as a high person, and while others are still thinking of their own problems, you will be thinking of new plans and ways to move forward. Great words can give you peace. Just one great word can erase thousands of negative words that you or someone else has spoken into your life. You do not need the words of others in your life. You have control of your life, and others do not have the power to control you. You are in charge!

Words you speak into your life can make you care for yourself and become tender towards yourself. You do not have to be harsh and judge yourself negatively. You do not have to think poorly of yourself. You should love yourself and treat yourself in the best way. Great words will do that for you. They can make you ignore those that act like enemies. You will not be bothered about those who are speaking or acting negatively towards you. Your mind will be clean, healthy, and filled with positive things. Even those that are planning to be your enemies will give up because they can see that what they do does not affect you.

Great words can make you bold, courageous, and forward-looking. You will have a higher expectation about yourself. You will not think low of yourself, and before you know it, you will be acting high. Big doors will open before you, and you will occupy great places.

Great words can affect your actions. Instead of doing wrong things, you are likely to do positive things. You can never be on the wrong road with great words. You will only win and reach a higher level. The great words you speak into your life will change you into a different individual that will be set up for greatness in life.

Do not focus on what others say and think. You can't allow your self-celebration to be stopped by others' words and thoughts.

Chapter 19
The Things Others Say and Think

Do not feel moved by what people say or think about you. Do not allow the words of your friends, neighbours, and family members to disturb you; they do not own your life, and they don't have the right to convince you that you cannot celebrate yourself. They can't stop you. You can't close their mouths, but you have to celebrate you life. You must see yourself as the very best and then put your life on top.

There are people who speak lies into the lives of others. They are looking to convince that others aren't good enough. Don't listen to such people; move on with your own life. Your life is too precious for you to let it be mistreated because of someone's lack of understanding about you. You should always celebrate yourself.

Don't allow anyone to use his words to move you out of

your position. If someone does not appreciate you, it's not your fault, and you do not have to beg for him to appreciate you. As long as you value yourself and see yourself as someone precious and special, you should never give up. Keep going on and remember that the days ahead are going to be very special for you.

There are people that do not understand what you are thinking or what self-celebration is all about. When you are celebrating yourself, it will be very difficult for you to convey the message to them. They do not value themselves. If such people come near you, simply say in your mind, 'This is a lie, and I am not going to believe it.' Take courage, speak positive things into your own life, and enjoy your life celebration.

You can never give up on your life because of what someone said to you. Why should you depend on the words of a human being? Why should you try to find the value of yourself in the words that someone says to you? Why should you lose your hope because of others? You have to create your own words and use them to win against the situation. You have the power to switch your life to a road of fine things and great celebration.

You have to begin now to manage your own world. Don't allow the words of others to manage it for you. Choose to win, to stay strong, and to connect to the power of love that lies on the inside of you. Make great choices for your life that befit your true image. Go for a winning life that will bring lots of celebration your way. Always keep your courage and know that you are doing the best. Don't depend on other people.

Many people lead selfish lives and do not care about others; you may meet people like that in your journey. They do not know about self-celebration and do not celebrate their lives. They are used to the old and negative feelings. Ignore such people. You do not have to be disturbed about their attitudes; don't allow your mind to be worried because of the bad things that they have released into your life. You still have to keep your smile and continue in self-celebration.

In the midst of people, you are an overcomer. No matter the words that they speak to you, they're not for you. You are not a small individual; you are a talented individual full of self-celebration. Some people do not carry a good presence and are very undermining; do not mind such people. You believe in what you think of yourself, which is positive and will rule over any negativity that others bring your way. Always be determined to win and keep your focus very strong. Don't allow anyone to delay you from getting the next blessing coming into your life.

There are a lot of good things that life has to offer you, and there are lots of things that you can do with your life. You do not have to depend on the words of people. Remember that you are very talented and special, and nothing is going to get in the way of that positive feeling that you hold towards yourself. Even the things that have not worked out for you in the past will work out soon. Everything is going to be okay, and you are going to reach a shining future.

Erase every bad word that anyone has spoken into your life. Never believe it or keep some of it for yourself. Create your own words that will give you the power to shine as you want. Follow your own path and make your own decisions to ensure that your future contains a successful story. Don't allow the words of people to rule over your life; don't let them destroy you with their contamination. You are too precious to look back or regret. You are too great for that mess. You have to shine. Don't allow people to say things to you that you do not believe. As long as you do not believe it, then don't tolerate it. Don't allow people to narrate your life or tell you what you are not. The good picture that you have in your heart regarding yourself should not be erased by another's inaccurate words. You have to stand firm like someone that knows what he or she is talking about. Fight for your life by making sure that you only allow the flow of positive words.

Sometimes the words that people speak to us can be very offending. It really hurts, and I understand how it feels. Some people just feel like talking, and they end up saying what they should not say. It doesn't show on their outside, but on their inside they know that they have said the wrong things and aren't right. They know you are better than what they have said. They know you have come a long way, yet they still want to pollute your achievements through their negativity. Don't give room for people like that in your life.

In case no one has told you this before, you are doing a great job. You are excellent, and your attitude is great. You are working hard at your workplace, and you are doing the best for your life. You are on the right path in life and you are going to excel. You are going to blossom like a beautiful flower. Your life is going to be filled with lots of self-celebration, and you are going to march with pride to your destiny. You are on the right road!

People have different styles of speaking. Some people are too hard on others when they speak. They tend to always correct you, but they never remember to celebrate you for the little right things you do. In life, the little things are more important than the big things, and you should always appreciate people that honour you for those little things you do every day.

There is nothing wrong in someone correcting you, but anytime they correct you, you will always feel as if there is something that you haven't done right, and that brings a sense of incompleteness. It can also take away your joy. I want you to know that you are very great at the little things that you do right. You should celebrate yourself and put yourself on high. You deserve something special and spontaneous. You deserve a 'well done' and a round of applause because you are at your best. You should always use encouraging words towards yourself. Look for something good to say to yourself. Celebrate yourself for every time you try something. See yourself as someone useful and good. Always see the treasure and the greatness that lies the inside of you. Value the things that you do and be proud of yourself. Always be happy, and do not allow the words of others to hurt you. Don't allow anyone to put you down. Words cannot kill you or stop you from doing the things that you want. Words are powerful, but you can choose to deny ones that are not useful. I see you as a winner and believe that your greatest days are ahead of you. You are going to come out very strong, and you are going to overcome your challenges. Everything will be okay with you. You will not be shy – you will be bold like a lion.

I do understand that you can be weighed down by the words that someone speaks into your life. You probably wish that the person will tell you wonderful words, but instead you keep hearing things that make you feel you are imperfect. Stay in your own beliefs and see yourself based on your perspective. Don't allow anyone to take your courage or make you lose your focus. Don't let them get in the way.

I urge you today to realise that you are better than what others say. You have so much capability and talent. You have the capacity to achieve something greater. You are filled with inner know-how. You know the way to take, and you are very intelligent. You are truly willing to become somebody in life, and you will become it. You are on the right side and will get to your desired destination soon.

Some people might want you to be like them, but you have to choose not to, especially if they say negative things about you. There are people that are ready to talk you out of your dreams; don't listen to them. Listen to the ones who talk you *into* your dreams, who inspire and elevate you on a daily basis. Don't allow anyone to make you lose the hope within you. You don't have to be like them; be yourself, because that's what is right for you.

You might have close friends that want you to settle for second best because that is what they think. Do not mind them. You are the only one who knows what is best for you, so do not settle for second best. Someone might say to you, 'You are too young,' or, 'You are too old.' Do not mind them and go for what you want. Keep planning and acting towards becoming what you want in life. Keep your head up high. Keep believing that you will be the best one day.

Do not allow people to use their personal lives to define yours. Maybe those that have achieved what you want tell you that it is not easy to achieve it. Ignore them. Don't allow anything or any words to limit you. You are unstoppable. You can get to wherever you want to get in life. They might have experienced difficulty, but when it is your turn, you might not experience any. Even in the difficult places you can still make it and come out as the best.

Some people create disturbing things in life. They are not always going to be perfect; they are likely to inconvenience us and sometimes make our lives miserable. It is normal, and we have to understand that. People are not always going to do things in the way we expect. They aren't going to go out of their way to please us or make us feel better. They aren't always going to hope something better for us. They aren't going to tell us the perfect words that we want to hear. However, protect yourself by saying something beautiful to yourself every day, because you are going to make it. I want you to know that you are going to be a very great individual, and you are going to overcome your life challenges. You are going to step out as someone great. You will achieve higher levels compared to the ones that you have experienced before. You are going to get better things for your life. You are going to be huge in this life in terms of your achievement. You are going to be a famous person, and your bad past is going to be over. You are going to move on to enjoy the very best that life has in store for you.

The negative words other people say about you cannot define your life. It doesn't tell me who you are; I will only know who you are by the good things you do, and I will appreciate you for them. I do not have the time to focus on the negative things that people say about you. I know people can be very crazy at times and misjudge people; they turn a blind eye to the good others are doing. You are more powerful than that, and you are likely to be stronger as you prepare for a greater future.

People cannot declare your future. Your actions will define your future. The negative words that people speak to you have nothing to do with where you are going in life; those words are just like rubbish, and you should throw them into the bin. Don't carry them with you or embrace them in anyway. Lift yourself up and stand tall against the negative words of people. You are an overcomer. You are bigger than your challenges and will defeat those negative words through your powerful, right actions. You are going to win, and there will be something awesome in your future.

Some people do not love themselves. They hate themselves and are not happy about anything that has to do with their lives. You can't change them, and your words can't make them anything better. Therefore, do not focus on them. Focus on yourself and allow your life to be about what comes from inside of you. Have something to celebrate about and know that in your future you will celebrate even more.

Acknowledge your potentials; using them will give you a lot to celebrate.

Chapter 20
Not Acknowledging
Your Potentials

The word 'potential' refers to talents and abilities that are not fully used or realised. If you do not acknowledge your potentials, you will be unable to celebrate yourself. You have to look on the inside of yourself and check the potential you have. Your potential makes your life easy and gives you a reason to celebrate yourself. Have you ever wondered why people like David Beckham celebrate themselves every day and are celebrated by the world? It is because they have realised their potential and make use of it.

People that bury their potential do not enjoy life; they usually feel like they are living for nothing. Use your potential to create a positive sense of life. I referred to potential earlier as talents and abilities. Your talents and abilities give you a sense of happiness because they make you natural and help you to express yourself naturally. Your talents and abilities are what you have to offer the world. You must believe that you have big potential and that you are going to use it in a big way. You are about to step up to use your potential in a unique way, and it is going to make the world proud of you. Your name is going to be big because of your potential. Your day of little beginnings will no longer be remembered because of your large potential. You are going to step up and remain high forever.

There is no doubt that these gifts are still inside of you. Some of your friends might have noticed it; if they are brave enough, they will tell you about it. Not everyone will tell you what your gifts are. You should always appreciate people that remind you of your gifts and talents. Do not sit there watching others use their gifts while you remain in silence – use your gifts, too! Your assignment on earth is to fulfil your destiny, and that involves using your talents and gifts. You are not going to die with your talents and gifts; you are going to use them in order to shine. You are going to use them to get known and to fly high. You'll be big regardless of your inner weaknesses and imperfections.

By using your gifts and talents, you will be able to touch many lives. If you have a constant desire to do something positive, then do it. Don't hide your face from the crowd;

let them see your face and what you have to offer. Your gifts and talents are treasures that are more precious than gold. The ideas you have cannot be wasted and are there to make you great.

You are like God. God is powerful and you are powerful. You can't live an average life because you do not deserve it. You deserve something high, something precious. You deserve to be known and to walk with great people. The sky is your limit, and maybe you can even fly above the sky. You are a supernatural being that is able to release great things in this world, enabling people to respect you.

Your intelligence is what will make you to succeed in life. You can reach out for higher levels beyond your imagination. You were created to excel and shine above others. Do not be satisfied with what you've achieved before; there is more you can do. You have to believe that you have what it takes in the midst of people. See yourself as a gifted person.

People may have tried to push you down and make you think that you are useless. Don't mind them. To your surprise you may find out that you are even better than them. You don't have to go about looking sad, like someone who has finished life. Your disappointments do not affect your potential; you still have a brighter future ahead of you. You are going somewhere far, and there is a lot that life has in store for you.

Your potential is going to put you together for greatness. It is going to make you walk in places that you haven't walked before. It is going to set you up for a special life. Your potential will add to your life and change your life history. Your potential helps you end up greater than you have ever been before.

Even people that are supporting you in your destiny might say things to you that they do not mean. You do not have to focus on it. Don't allow what they say to discourage you or make you lose interest in the place you are meant to go to with them. Your destiny is too precious to be destroyed by what people say. Sometimes the people on whom we rely and who give us the most of their time can let us down through their words. You have to know that people aren't always perfect, and sometimes they do give up. However, take care of yourself and make sure you do not give up. Keep going and mind your own destiny. You have something very great ahead of you, and you are going to have a very splendid life.

What others think about you is not the most important thing to you. People can believe wrong things about you; maybe it's because they do not know you very well, or it's because of an action from your past. However, that should not drive you to abandon your great belief in yourself. You have to believe that you are a person that deserves self-celebration. You are very special, and you have to hold on to your self-positive beliefs.

In life, people can easily reflect on something you have done in your past and decide not to love you for it. However, that should not be your focus. It's up to them to let go of what you have done and to choose to love you again. You can be nice towards them, but you can't force them to change. You have to keep shining with the little you have and make the best use of your day, so that when even those that you have wronged in the past hear about it, they will be shocked. They will not believe the difference you have made.

Anyone is free to think of anything one wants. If you have some people in your life that still think negatively about you and still remember your little days, you don't have to worry about that. Keep moving on with your life and ensure that you are making the best use of the opportunities that come your way. Enjoy your life and get the best out of it for your satisfaction. You have the right to live and excel as you wish. People might feel you do not deserve something in life, but as long as you feel you deserve it, then go for it.

Remember that it is you who matters the most. You have to keep yourself high and take care of everything that concerns you. You don't have to allow negative feelings to flow over you due to others' judgement. People do not have the final say over your life. You are great and are going to make it – that's the good news.

Maybe you have some side of you that you have not perfected yet, and when people consider that, they feel you do not deserve to achieve a certain goal. You do not have to be afraid or allow their decision to override your life. Be very bold and stand for yourself; let them know how great you are and communicate the fact that you are capable. You can keep on trying until it works.

If people assume that you aren't good enough, that doesn't mean you aren't good. Let them assume whatever they like. I want you to know that you are very special and are going to special places in life. You are going to be an individual that will be praised by many nations. You are going to be lifted and will stand high in life. If you believe me, you will begin to see yourself achieve these things.

People's negative assumptions can never stop your bright future or reduce who you are. They can't make you lower. You must have this full belief in yourself and rise to do what you haven't done before. Your life can be a source of entertainment to others by using your gifts and talents. You do not have to settle for lower things; you can achieve very great things and stand high.

There is a wise saying: 'Never judge a book by its cover.' If people are judging you by the cover in certain areas of your life, you need to keep your smile on, and don't allow what they do to make you lose your joy. You have to realise yourself that you have special gifts and talents. You know where you are coming from, and you know your capabilities. You know you are very able, so don't wait for them to qualify you. Qualify yourself. If people are sensing incorrect things about you, you don't have to be troubled about it. You know who you are, so keep on doing the good things that you are doing. Your good will put them to shame. Life is too valuable for you to start thinking and imagining the wrong things others are saying. Keep on running your own race. Your life will be very beautiful one day, and the grace you carry is going to change your life history forever.

You need to be willing to break free from your self-imposed limitations. Maybe a friend said to you, 'Do you really think you can do that? That opportunity is not for you.' That's a lie – don't believe in that. Even if you try and fail, at least you will know that you have done something. To your surprise, you might even fly higher if you do it, and it will be one of the best moments of your life. You are too precious to keep down.

Do not allow negative words to hurt you. If you are not careful, negative words can become a stronghold over your mind, and you won't feel free. You have the final authority over your life, and no person's negative words can win over you. Words are powerful, and you should play the tune of positive words, ignoring the old tunes of rubbish.

If you've been held back for years due to negative words that your parents, teachers, or peers have spoken, then it's time to get loose and set yourself free. Say positive statements such as, 'People like me.' Do not think people dislike you or are against you. Always speak great words and dream great. Enjoy what life has to offer you. Never give up, because it's your time to shine.

A friend of mine wanted to start a new project, and he spoke to a friend on the phone about it. The first thing the friend said was, 'It is a very tough project. it's not easy.' Then those words started playing in my friend's mind. I told him, 'Who told you that you cannot make it? Who told you that you were created to live an average life? Who told you that you are a loser? Don't mind those words – those words are not for you.'

Maybe you are looking forward to marriage, and someone told you that you are unattractive. It is a lie. You have to reject the lie and reach for the things that you want to happen in your life. There are always new things for each day, so do not allow the lies of others to steal your ability to tap into your best for the day. You are very great and will go far.

Move away from wrong environments.
Remember, what you see and feel
can affect your self-celebration.

Chapter 21
Staying in the Wrong Environments

Recently, I have seen people with great gifts and talents mingling with bad people. When I say bad people, I mean people that do not encourage others. You can be very excellent with your ability, but if you take it to the wrong people, they can steal it from you, and it will affect your joy. Do not allow anyone to steal your passion. Wrong environments do not empower you to be your best; rather, they discourage you. You do not have to stay in touch with everybody. You have to subtract the people that say you cannot make it. Such people remind you of your weaknesses and mistakes; they show you your imperfect sides and are not willing to take any action to bring the best out of you. They have not dealt with issues in their own lives, and they carry a load of unhappiness. You have to avoid such people and stay in environments that are happy. The surroundings you choose to stay in should soothe your gifts and talents, enabling you to feel free to express what you have to offer.

Environments that do not allow you to fulfil your potential must be ignored. You are focusing on how you are going to get to the next level. You have a project that you want to carry out. You are worried in a positive way about your dreams. You want to make things happen in life. Therefore, you do not need people who are settling for less. The kinds of friends you have tell me who you are and where you are going. You should move with people that have high energy and are willing to face challenges. You will easily catch their spirit and will be on your way to self-celebration. You will see that you also are capable. They will help you realise who you are and bring the best out in you.

Some environments do not cause you to flow or express yourself freely. These environments steal the talents of people and make them nothing. There are people that have no plans for their lives; you should not mingle with such people because they are only there to waste your time. They have nothing special to offer you and cannot escort you to your destination.

Certain environments are not helpful: you can shout for help, but no one will come. You have to disconnect from environments like that and connect to the ones that will provide the help you seek. Positive environments uplift you and give you a sound mind. Do not stay with people who are not ready to change and make your life better. Stay with mature individuals that know how to treat people right. Some people do not understand the principles of happy living; they are always sad and down. What do you think those people will do to you? Do you think they will affect you negatively? Yes, they will, because they are focused on their bad experiences. They will also treat you in the same way they treat themselves. They are not ready for happiness.

If you stay with people that do not understand the principles of self-celebration, then you will be unable to celebrate yourself. There are people that are living mentally unhealthy lives, and they have no clue about how they will come out of it because their minds are filled with negativity. Do not allow such people to get in the way of your self-celebration.

There are people who are willing to discourage themselves every day. Such people cannot promote your self-celebration. They are very strict, and anytime you go to them, they make you feel down. They do not inspire your joy. Try and stay far away from people like that, and keep away from environments that remind you of your past.

Environments that are frustrating do not encourage self-celebration. You can be at the right place but at the wrong time. If you are in the right place but at the wrong time, then you may meet people who will discourage you. You have to leave the place ahead of time.

Some environments have nothing to offer, and all you get is the same old stuff. Try to stay away from such environments. Self-celebration connects with the environment you are in, because you can only celebrate in positive environments. Environments that add extra to your destiny are the right ones for you, and you will value them. Stay in environments that draw you close to your destiny. If you are planning to be a singer, stay in environments where there are great singers; this will give you a lot of self-celebration because by watching them, you remind yourself that you will be in that position one day. You will be full of happiness and joy, and you will feel like you are on the same level as them.

Go to environments that remind you of good things. Simply watching a beautiful flower is sometimes better than watching some people. You need to keep your mind pure, so do not go to environments that will pollute your mind. You know that life is too precious to give a chance to something that will discourage you. Don't allow anything to contaminate the great things that are inside you.

Some environments make you feel a great sense of achievement. Make an effort to be in these places. The locations that make you feel worthy and remind you that you are a capable person are the right ones for you; they will increase your self-celebration and help you know that you are creditable and commendable.

Some environments appreciate you. The people there are grateful for your presence, they treat you well, and they are thankful for the kind of life you are living. They are glad about the things you have used your life, for and they are ready to stand for you and give you the best possible support. The people are always pleased to see you and believe in you greatly. They love everything about you and turn up with joy anytime they see you.

If you plant a banana tree in a small pot, its growth will be limited. The problem is not the banana tree – it's with the pot. The pot makes the environment. The environment is stifling growth. Your environment might not have the space to allow you use your talents and gifts, and if you can escape from such an environment, please do so. You need a place where you can climb up levels and grow into your dreams. That's why you always stretch better when you go through difficulties. Difficulties enable you to move into the right environment, which will facilitate your dreams. If you've stepped into a bigger and more successful environment before, and suddenly the door did close, don't worry – there is a bigger one ahead of you. You will get into a bigger one that will give you the space to shine greater than you ever have.

You should be happy when environments make you uncomfortable. Your lack of comfort is likely to make you go for better environments, where greater things will happen to you. Rejection and disappointment often lead you to a better environment. When someone chooses not to give you the response you are looking for within a specific environment, you are likely to search for new environments, and that will bring something better out of you.

Maybe you have not experienced favour in a former environment.; I am here to tell you there is a lot of favour in the environments ahead of you. There is something beautiful and amazing waiting for you; you are going to climb higher and taste new things. You are going to be liked by everybody, and you are going to be embraced and treated better than you have been before.

People that stay in negative environments do not excel. You have to make an effort to come out of a bad environment. An environment that cannot tolerate your nature is not a good environment for you. If you stay with people that do not carry great dreams like the ones you carry, they are likely to press your dreams down and will not understand what you are up to. You need like-minded people as friends so that you and them can rub energy together to create something beautiful.

You need to stay in healthy, positive, and faith-filled environments that are suitable for you and that give room for you to display your good side, qualities, gifts, and talents. You need environments that will increase your confidence and push you to achieve greater. You need environments that will improve your self-trust and help you see the beautiful dreams that you have on the inside.

Imagine someone planting a good seed in bad soil: the seed won't take root and grow. You don't have to plant yourself in the bad soil. Bad soil represents the bad people and bad environments that can get in the way of your destiny. You should always stay in good places that will keep you as the first-class and high-quality person you are. You should stay with people that will make you feel superior and excellent every day of your life.

People that abuse you physically, emotionally, mentally, and verbally are not good people. You should stay away from people like that. Do not be afraid to leave such environments – leave them quick. You were not created to be mistreated and abused. You should not allow yourself to be ill-treated in any way. You should not allow others to misuse you or exploit you. Don't stay with people that are always manipulating and using others to negative advantages. There is nothing wrong with feeling superior but when a person uses it to misuse others something is wrong with it.

Don't allow anyone or any environment to hide your gifts and talents. Make sure that you come out with your true nature wherever you are. Don't allow environments to put out of sight what you have. Always make use of the opportunities that come your way in whatever environment you find yourself. Do not keep what you have to offer the world as a secret – show them that you have some things in store.

I have seen people with big talents hide them due to the kind of authority they are with. They are very afraid to use their skills at work or amidst people; they feel that they would not be appreciated or rewarded for it, and that no one likes what they have to offer. Sometimes people lose their speciality when they are in the midst of people, and they forget who they really are. Do not allow such a thing to happen to you; always look ahead and keep shining even in the smallest places.

There is a special destiny in you, and it's not yet complete. You have to complete it by nurturing it every day. You have to accomplish those dreams that are lying inside you. It's not there for the show on the inside of you; it's there because it has to come out and become a reality. You have to execute your destiny by showing people a great sample of what you can do. You have to release the gifts and talents that are on your inside and use them to be a blessing to others.

Feel free to use your gifts and talents wherever you find yourself. Do not allow any environment to dominate you; instead, dominate the environment. Do not allow the inconveniences that wrong environments create to stop you from taking advantage of the moment. You can do it, too. You deserve to reach the maximum in life. You are not going to achieve the ordinary in life – you will achieve the extraordinary. Say to yourself, 'I am able to make it wherever I find myself in life. Nothing is going to stop me. I am going to break free from the limitations that lie inside of me.' I know you are very capable and one of the very best. I know you will go far in life. You will be doing a lot of significant things throughout your life, and you are going to grow taller beyond any barrier that can stop you.

Do not reside in environments that cannot aid your destiny. Such environments are likely not to assist you and your mind in planning for the future. You will not be able to think clearly and see the future in environments that are stifling. Instead, stay in environments that will encourage you to see the bigger picture. Environments that will help you to think ahead and dream bigger are the best. Environments that will serve your destiny and celebrate it are the ones you need.

**Give your dreams a new beginning.
Your fresh start erases the past and
gives you something to celebrate.**

Chapter 22
Not Giving Your Dreams
a New Beginning

You can start again. Your dreams are not going to die; they will succeed, and you will get to wherever you want in life. If you allow the disappointments of yesterday to stop you, you will not be able to stretch higher. You can regain your focus and achieve your dreams with hard work. Your yesterday is over, and today is a new day for you. You are going to make it.

A fresh start will empower you to do the things you haven't done before. It will help you to regain yourself and dream big. You will be able to activate the desires of your heart and take the right actions to make them happen. A fresh start will motivate you because you will be able to do things in a new way; you will be able to see yourself become a big and mighty person that will always be on top.

Your dreams are very special and connect to your future.

Your future is more important than your disappointments. You can make great plans of what you want the future to look like. Your dreams are very significant, and only you know them well. You are greater than the things you've been through in the past. You should always be keen and excited about the future, because that is where the good things lie for you. Why should you give up now? Why would you look back? Why do you want to lose your hope? There are still a lot of awesome things in this world for you; you simply haven't discovered them yet. You are going to have great reasons to celebrate yourself in the future. You are going to step into levels and zones you haven't stepped into before. You are going to have a lot to enjoy, and your life will never be the same.

Sometimes dreams fail to happen despite your best efforts. You simply have to create a new beginning. Your dreams will give birth to new things and will make your life more interesting. Never give up on your dreams in life. I know a man that tried two thousand times before his dream came to past. He kept going despite his failures.

I want you to know that you are going to succeed. You are going to fly into the sky in the future. You are going to achieve extraordinary things that will show you how capable you are. The accomplishments of your tomorrow are going to be very beautiful. You will gain your victory and become an awesome person in this world. You will do what you have never done before.

Every day is a new day and it comes with new opportunities that you should not miss. Tap into those new opportunities. I hear you saying, 'I have lost my dreams.' Let me tell you, your dreams are not lost – they are just in the preparation stage. Your dreams have something to offer which no one else can offer, apart from you. That's what makes you a very special person.

In life, you need people in order to succeed, and there are people out there who have good hearts and are willing to tell you how great you are. I hope that you will meet people who will assist you, inspire you, bless you, motivate you, quicken you, protect you, energise you, upgrade you, increase you, listen to you, walk with you, wait with you, encourage you, stir you, and celebrate with you.

You desire that your dreams will achieve higher things for you. Speak into your life words such as 'I am well able', 'I am great', 'I am blessed', and 'I will see my dreams come to pass'. Do not focus on the lies that your mind says to you; don't allow your inner limitations to win your fight to make your life a better one. There might be obstacles opposing your dreams, but you will make it. You might be feeling empty on the inside regarding your dreams, but I can assure you that it's not over. You might not receive much from your efforts, but there is much in your future. There are greater things ahead of you, and you are going to experience lovely times. You will be restored to the extent that you will even forget your pain and all the bad things you have experienced in the past. You need to hope that things will get better in the future. You have to keep dreaming until those dreams become a reality. Refresh your mind and know that your dreams will come true. Keep reminding yourself that you have a gift on the inside, and that gift will spell you in the future.

Great people go through challenges before getting to their destinies. It's normal; we cannot avoid problems in life. The world may be trying to push your dreams down, but those dreams belong to you. Those dreams are going to make you big in this world and prove to the world that you are a winner. No one can steal your dreams. Your dreams produce your uniqueness, because no one can do it like you.

You should keep your smile on regarding your dreams; believe even when others do not. How you start does not matter, but how you finish does matter. The end of your dreams is better than the beginning. Do not despise humble beginnings. You may start humble and small, but your future will shine like an amazing light.

Keep pushing yourself towards your dreams. Get your dreams back and try something new. Carry out those dreams in a new way. You will see that things will begin to change immediately when you start fresh. If you do not want to continue with the dreams you had in the past, you can come up with new ones; by the time you regain your focus, you will see that the things that you have lost in the past will return to you. You will end up smiling and thanking yourself that you did not give up. You have to play your path and let the rest work out. A little focus towards your dream will make a difference. People might have treated you badly in the past, and this can make your dreams dormant, but I advise you to try again.

I can hear you saying, 'The actions that I have taken in the past have destroyed my future.' It is not over yet; rid yourself of those thoughts, because the hurt and pain you are experiencing are not going to destroy your future. Do not place your dreams on hold due to negative thoughts; life gives you a lot of chances. If you are sitting there thinking there are no more chances, or you say to yourself, 'It's finished,' I am here to tell you that it is *not* finished because there are a lot of chances for you to still get it right.

You will be happy about your dreams in the future because you can take a fresh start and come up with new, creative ideas. Quit talking about the past and start talking about the future. Start talking about the great things that are going to happen to you. Start talking about the wonderful experiences that are ahead of you. Leave the bad things alone and plan for something great.

A fresh start is important. You can start all over again. If you do not give your dreams a new beginning, you will be left with the same old stuff. You have to allow the old to pass away, and then you can give yourself a new start. Stop looking back at past disappointments; they cannot do you any good. Every day is fresh, and there are better things compared to what was in your yesterday. Your future has many good things in store. It holds precious things, but it is waiting for the right time so that it can commence. Your future is specially designed for you, and it has what it takes to meet your needs. You will be taken care of in the future, so you don't have to be troubled about the future. Do not give up on yourself, because you are about to step into one of the best moments of your life. The seed of greatness that is inside you is going to produce a river of love that will heal many nations. Many people will discover their destinies through you. They will see pictures of their lives and dreams clearly because of you. Your success will inspire many and will tell them never to give up on themselves. There will be hope in the world because of you.

The seeds of greatness that you carry are not a waste of time – they are the things that will make your future big. Most of the seriously talented people in the world have been through bad experiences such as abuse, divorce, and more. You cannot let what you have been through hold you back. I know what you have been through is unfair, but the action you take today has the chance to erase your yesterday. The world knows that you are carrying great gifts and talents, and it cannot stop you from producing your best today. You have to say to yourself, 'I am full of can-do power.' There are people with multiple talents; maybe you are one of them. You can rise today and start using your talents.

You have to stir up the gift within you. If you've buried your talents behind depression or disappointments, it is time for you to rise. You can start fresh today and overcome your challenges. Your great qualities should not be ignored; they should be used to bring out the best in you. They should take you far and cause your life to shine against all odds.

A new thing is about to happen in your life, and you have to create the room for it. Can you perceive what is about to happen in your life? You have to give room to the new thing in your thinking. You have to think that it is possible. You have to think that you are able to achieve your goals. Maybe you have nothing today, and you think it's over. By the time you start giving room to new things in your thinking, you will see that you will end up with something, and it will never be over in your life. Maybe you have a lot of problems in your life that are weighing you down. Start thinking of a new thing, and it will manifest. Do not limit your thinking – think higher, think of something different. Imagine walking in great places and meeting very great people. Everything is possible for you! Don't allow the things that are weighing you down to get in the way of your success.

Dust yourself off and separate from your past. If you cannot find someone to encourage you, learn to encourage yourself by speaking powerful words into your life. Say to yourself, 'I've come too far to stop now.' The truth is that you've been through a long journey, and you've achieved something, but there is even more in your future. Don't allow 'good enough' to be enough; there are always better things in life, and you will find them by searching.

Keep believing in the things you are expecting to happen in your life. Maybe a relationship did not work out as you thought, but you can still come up with a new plan to make new friends. You can still move on and get lots of things done. Encourage yourself in a positive direction. Pick yourself up and walk into great places to make things happen.

There are always many chances for you to redeem your mistakes. You simply have to try to make things work out, and you will see that they will work to your advantage. There are a lot of opportunities waiting out there for you. There are a lot of ways that you can make it through life. There are a lot of people waiting to hear from you and willing to help you become what you want to become. You don't need to give up; you can start again. You can build a stronger foundation for yourself and your future because you are about to start from the beginning. You can take a look at where you are going again; you can research what works and what doesn't so that you can focus on the areas where you can produce your best. You can create a strong ground for your dreams by building in the right places.

You can establish yourself again despite the things you have lost in life. You can establish your family with focus and understanding. You can reach out to others with the new life you are about to start for yourself. You can start an example of re-establishment for others to follow. You can gain back the things you have lost. Stand strong and walk in the path that will lead to your success and celebration in life. You can make it, and it's never too late for you.

If you have high self-esteem, you will be filled with reasons to celebrate yourself.

Chapter 23
Low Self-Esteem

Do you know that you are high? Being high means having a high self-esteem. Someone like you, who has been through a lot in life and has come a long way, deserves to have high self-esteem. I am sure that those who appreciate you will want you to be high and on top. They will want you to be standing well and not holding negative doubts regarding yourself.

If you are currently experiencing low self-esteem, you are about to come out of it. You are going to step into a place of self-discovery, which will make you think highly of yourself, and the way you carry yourself will change. Your opinion of yourself will become different. You will feel good on the inside, and you will be excited and bold about yourself every day.

High self-esteem involves you having a high regard about yourself. It has nothing to do with you considering yourself to be wrong or passing negative judgements on yourself. You simply have to love yourself and be zealous about where you are going in life; this starts by having a high self-esteem.

Low self-esteem can stop you from celebrating yourself. It can make you feel like you aren't good enough and will deny you of the happiness you hold towards yourself. It will make you think that others are better. It will deny you of the self-celebration you should create when you do little things that are good. I want you to be happy, and you can only be happy when something positive is going on inside of you. You should always think about the good things you do. Don't focus on the bad or imperfect things. Appreciate yourself anytime you do the smallest thing to help another person. Feel good about it and say to yourself, 'I have done something great today.' By doing so, you will think highly of yourself, which will help build your self-esteem. This process will give you something good to remember for the day.

If you keep listening to what others are thinking of you, you will have low self-esteem. People will always be people, and the funny thing is, people are full of strange characteristics. What can we do about that? People might be assessing you wrongly despite all your efforts to do things right, but you do not have to focus on that. Instead, focus on yourself and keep doing the great things that you are doing. You are in charge of yourself.

How do you evaluate the things that you have done in the past? Do you give yourself a good evaluation? Do you think you have tried? If yes, that's good. If no, you have to try to give a good evaluation about yourself at all times. Even when you fail, you can rise up again. You have the chance to become the very best. You have to see the outcomes in the different areas of your life as good ones – even when something fails completely. You should always celebrate yourself. Say to yourself, 'I have done well.' Call others together to celebrate yourself. Tell them about how good you are; help them to focus on the good areas of your life. Get them excited about you and laugh. Show them that you are very capable. Give them the room to see your talents and gifts, helping them to see you in a new way. Get together with your friends and make it a point to celebrate yourself.

How do you view the areas in which you need to make improvements? Do you feel you are too messy to get yourself together? Do you say that others are better than you? Do you say to yourself, 'I blew it off,' or do you say, 'I did try, and next time I will do better'? Do not say you blew it off, because you deserve praise for every time you try. You should always lift yourself up into achieving higher levels.

What sort of belief do you have about yourself? Think about that for a second. Do you say to yourself, 'I am worthy,' or do you say, 'I am unworthy'? You have to choose the right words for yourself and call yourself perfect even when you are not. You have to get a different picture of your life and still carry yourself high, even in places where you have fallen.

I want you to have good emotions inside of yourself, because that's the only thing that will make you celebrate yourself. You don't have to focus on the negative things; you do not have to cry when you make a mistake. You can still laugh and say, 'I know I will do better. Watch me – I'm on the way to my destiny.' I want you to feel good about yourself and think of yourself as somebody special. Always value yourself and think of yourself as a person of honour.

How do you see yourself in the midst of people? Do you feel that you are competent? If not, you have to start seeing yourself as competent, starting today. How do you judge your behaviour? Do you wish you were someone else? I do not want you to feel like you can be someone else. I want you to believe in yourself! I want you to appreciate yourself.

I want you to believe that your behaviour is great and very suitable. How do you feel when you make mistakes? Do you allow your conscience to fight you because of your mistakes? You do not have to allow that. You should see your mistake as a step towards your greatness. Mistakes are normal – we all make them. You don't have to feel like you have destroyed a good principle when you make a mistake. You do not have to feel like you have gone against good ethics. I know you will do it right the next time.

There might be issues in your childhood that are affecting your self-esteem. You simply have to forget what has happened in your childhood. Do not remember the past anymore. You will soon be healed from the hurt of your childhood. The bitter things that you experienced in your early days cannot compare to that next step you are about to take to make your life a better one. Focus on what is next and let the past heal itself.

Stars are people that had an uneasy childhood; maybe their parents did not provide for them well or were simply not there for them. That never stopped stars from becoming great people and winners. They still made it and proved to the world that the best was inside of them. Problems only bring the best out in you. Why not use your problem to show your cleverness, by learning to overcome any negativity that comes out of your childhood?

I want you to love yourself. Feel affection towards yourself. Adore yourself in a great way. Dress great to show how wonderful you are. Be in love with yourself and be devoted to letting people know that you are the best. Be positive about yourself and build a very stronger inner being, which will cause you to celebrate yourself every day. Never give up. The opinion you hold about the type of person you are really matters, so hold the best opinion about yourself. You have to think highly of yourself and believe that you are capable. You must know that you can shine like others. You can achieve the great things that others have achieved. See yourself on a road where others will also be able to see the best in you. You have to always see great things in yourself.

You know that life is not easy. When you are faced with a problem, do you start saying negative things about yourself? You don't have to, and you don't need to. Don't be afraid of problems — always see them as something you can overcome. You can always stand strong and smile despite your problems in life. You should remember that your value matters, and you should not bring yourself down in any way. You're worth a lot more than what you have been through. You're worth more than what life is giving you at the moment. You're worth something special. You are great; you aren't cheap at all. I rate you as first because I know you have what it takes to be the best.

You should not allow anything in the world to change the positive view you have for yourself, and you have to prove to people that you are thinking positively about yourself. Hold a beautiful and wonderful view about yourself. Speak nice things about yourself and keep your heart tender and loving. The greatest love in life is the one you have for yourself. Love yourself and show the world that you are of a high value.

You can pretend to be confident even if you aren't feeling like it. Before you know it, everyone will believe you; they will start shouting your name and will run to you. If you lose your job, will you allow it to knock your confidence down? The answer is no. There are a lot of jobs out there, and the next time you try, you will get a better one.

If you have been having low self-esteem, there is still time for you to change it to high self-esteem. The low self-esteem eating you on the inside is not going to remain there forever. You are going to change and become someone stronger with great self-belief. You will get your balance back and make your confidence regular; you will be on the way to celebrating yourself.

If you want mental health, you have to practise high self-esteem. If you want your mind to be in the best condition, you have to have high self-esteem. If you want to be okay psychologically, you have to gain high self-esteem. You will not be able to cope with stress properly if you have low self-esteem. I know you will overcome your low self-esteem with time; you will get better and possibly become the best.

Your nature has a lot to do with your self-esteem. Maybe you have a natural way of thinking and seeing things, and if you do not meet the set standard in your mind, then you feel that you aren't capable. That's not the way it should be. You should still think well of yourself, even if you have made mistakes. It takes practise to become perfect, and you will be perfect soon.

If you have low self-esteem, then instead of being relaxed when a new situation comes up, you feel pressured. Even if others tell you not to think that way, it will very hard for you to change. That's why self-esteem is about how you feel on the inside. You don't have to sense wrong things about yourself, because things have not gone the way you expect. When wrong things happen, it does not mean you are wrong. In order to keep high self-esteem, you have to protect yourself against negative experiences and leave environments that have a negative effect on you. Some environments can be very disturbing and do not have peace. You do not deserve to be in environments like that. You should remove yourself from environments like that, or remove the person that is causing the environment to be like that. You have to defend yourself in life and not allow any environment to steal your happiness.

You have to build your resilience. Resilience is the ability to return to a happy, positive state after a bad event. It is not easy to build resilience, but we all build it little by little. Try to work on your resilience so that you will be able to resist the things that can bring down your self-esteem. In life you need a strong foundation that helps you do what you want and achieve what you want.

Overcoming an abuse is not easy. If you have been abused sexually, emotionally, or physically, I understand that this will affect your self-esteem. I want you to try to look for something happy to do. Do things that will occupy your mind with happiness so that you will not have the time to remember those events.

There are a lot of happy things you can do with your life that can erase your past. Maybe your physical and emotional needs were neglected in childhood. I want you to say to yourself, 'Now I am going to take care of myself in the best way. I'll even be an example to those that are currently suffering the same situation.'

I understand that some situations are difficult to heal, and

I am here to help you overcome them. I understand the way you feel and how you have been eaten up by low self-esteem. It's not easy for you to get rid of it. It will take time to heal. Above all, I know you are going to win over it, and you will come out to be an elevated and self-motivated person.

Parents are very powerful. Some parents have spoken bad things into the lives of their children during childhood. The home is not always easy when we do not meet the expectations of our parents. If you find yourself in this situation, I want you to know that one day you will be a parent yourself. I want you to shake off that experience and say to yourself, 'My past is over, and I am about to step into my future.' You have to move on.

Recently I spoke to people that felt like they were the odd ones at school. They did not feel like others. Maybe their parents did not have enough money to buy them nice things. I also felt that way when I was at school. I was intelligent but did not feel the way others felt. Most of the students that allegedly feel good about themselves go through bitter experiences at home. I want you to know that you are great and beautiful, and people are looking for the opportunity to meet you. You are going to go far in life, and nothing has the power to stop you. Moving on might be painful, but you should do it anyway. You are still going to shine, so the past will not touch you. The past has nothing to do with where you are going. You will be bigger than you have ever been. Maybe, some of those that treated you oddly at school did not even have the confidence to face you. It does not mean they don't like you. Maybe they just thought you were too clever or too good to deserve their time. It's not your fault when people do not mix with you or talk with you. There is a lot more to your life than thinking about what others have done.

Your community is also important in terms of your self-esteem. Maybe you have experienced discrimination or prejudice in your community; you were not treated like the majority. I know that is not a good feeling, but you can still set yourself as an example. Say to yourself, 'It might not look like they are noticing me, but one day someone will notice me, and the people that have seen me in the community will speak good of me. I have lived a good life, and I have set an example.'

If you are poor but living in a wealthy neighbourhood, say to yourself, 'Very soon I am going to be rich, and this will pass away. I am not going to stay poor forever; I am going to make it one day, and I am going to get a better job. I know the best comes last, yet I am still going to stay awake and full of energy. I will even be happier than the ones that have lots of money, so I have nothing to miss out on.'

If you have experienced bullying or pressures at work, you are better off leaving that kind of work and looking for another job. Do not allow yourself to endure bad things when there are better alternatives. Bullying at work can affect your self-esteem, and it will be very difficult to celebrate yourself in such a situation. You were not created to be bullied; you were created to be loved and pampered.

You might have a health problem that has troubled you and made you feel like you are not part of the group. You can still apply wisdom and add excellence to even the smallest things you do. You will see that people will notice you, and your self-esteem will be high. Your sickness is unable to stop you from going far. Try whatever you can, and no matter how small it is, know that you have done something great for yourself and your community.

Bereavement can also affect your self-esteem. If someone that is very important to you has died, and if you have been trusting in this person, I know you might be afraid to face the world alone. However, try to move on, and very soon you will get a new relationship that will help build that bridge of love. You will end up stronger than before, and you will be a mentor to other weak ones.

Do not think that you are ugly or unattractive whereas others are more talented, intelligent, and interesting than you. You are the best, and I believe your best days are ahead. You are too precious to undermine yourself and to treat yourself that way. You are more worthy and prized than that. You are loved and are very important, and you are going to get things done.

Low self-esteem can stop you from fulfilling your potential. Maybe you are thinking of trying a new project, activity, or job. If you feel insecure, you will not be able to try it; you will discourage yourself from doing it. You will procrastinate until others go ahead of you. Don't be a viewer – be a partaker. A viewer only sees people doing things, but a partaker engages in those activities. Partakers have high self-esteem, and I want you to have high self-esteem to go for whatever you want in life.

Low self-esteem can make you tolerate abusive situations and relationships. When you feel insecure, you will look for a place to hide yourself. Get out of that insecurity and stand up for yourself. Stand as a great person and let great things follow you. Your life is very special, so do not give room for contamination. Abusive situations and relationships only leave you on a poor and painful edge. You must respect yourself and stay out of abusive zones.

Do not stay unhappy. Happiness connects with self-celebration. Start doing the things that make you happy now.

Chapter 24
Unhappiness

Happiness is a mental or emotional state of well-being characterised by positive or pleasant emotions, including contentment and joy. You do not deserve to be sad; instead, you should be very happy and focused. The happiness in you should drive you to do anything you want; it should make your life full of good things and satisfaction.

Unhappiness makes you feel unpleasant about yourself. Unhappiness is not a good thing because it leaves you hiding and feeling small. You are too special to be sad – you should always be happy and energetic. Fight and stand for your happiness. Be determined to live each day in a happy way. There is nothing better than a happy and zealous life. Unhappiness makes you feel dissatisfied about your achievements. You should be very proud of yourself; you should feel great about every little thing you do in life. Carry a smile and tell yourself that you are amazing and special, especially when you try. Every time you try, you deserve praise. You do not need to wait for others to do it for you; do it for yourself and make yourself happy. Rise up today and realise that you deserve happiness in this life. Put away the things that make you sad and discover the special things that lie inside you. Go up and announce to yourself that you have made up your mind to live a happy life. Remind yourself that you have decided to live this special new life, which is more interesting and far better than the one you had been living before.

Mount up with the wings of happiness and know that each day is going to be the best. Do whatever you want, and know that you can make your day very happy. Don't allow others to control or rule over you in a wrong way; instead, lead yourself and win with a big smile. That's what happiness is all about. Don't you know that you deserve a happy life? You do, and you should never lose your happiness in life. Make up your mind that you are going to focus on the things that make you happy and follow the path of happiness. Begin to see a happy you. See yourself in a new way. Believe that it is possible for you to live each day feeling very happy. Climb up; do not stay small or short. Get a bit higher, think higher, and dwell on the great things. Don't allow anything to stop you. Get yourself together for a happy life. Learn the things that make you happy and go for them every day of your life. It's high time you discover that the ingredients for a happy life lie on the inside of you; you can be the happiest person in this world.

You have to remove from your life the things that do not make you happy. Do not focus on the things that make you unhappy; instead, focus on the things that make you happy. If you are unhappy, you cannot celebrate yourself. Do not stay around people or places that make you unhappy. Do not get involved with events that make you sad. You know what makes you feel high and happy, so go for those things and have a lot of fun in your life.

Being optimistic involves having the most hopeful view about oneself or something; it's about having a positive attitude. Optimism and happiness are related because if you are very positive about most of the things in your life, then you will be happy. When bad things happen, do not sit down and start crying. Get up and switch on your happiness! Stay on the happy side and not on the sad side. Be very hopeful and know that your life can produce a lot of happiness; then you can start celebrating yourself. You have to feel a sense of satisfaction in order to be happy in life. You do not have to concentrate on the bad side of things; instead, get a sense of satisfaction on the inside and be pleased with yourself. Be positive even when you make mistakes. See yourself high even when you feel low.

Think of yourself as a very special and unique person, even when things do not work out as you expect. Always believe in yourself and keep going. Carry yourself like someone who is very pleased about himself or herself. Don't throw yourself down.

Do not assume that the world is against you. The world is for you and on your side. People are waiting out there to help you and to love your dreams. They will be interested about where you are going in life. There are people that would love to see your face every morning and get encouraged by looking into your eyes. Be happy and do not think that everything is over. You are just about to start!

You are in this world to succeed, so mount up with wings and fly. You are not a loser; you haven't wasted your time. Everything you have been through is only a preparation towards where you are going. You are going to land well in your destiny. You will be safe and will enjoy the good things that life has in store for you. You are not here by mistake. The world needs you in order to succeed and become a greater place, so be happy because you are discovering who you are.

A feeling that the world is against you can be caused by disappointments in your past. I do not know the disappointment you have been through, but I know that you are a winner and you are about to get to the next level. I know you aren't going to be ashamed in this life. However, you must look over your disappointments and say to yourself, 'I am moving on.' The fact that you have started something badly does not mean it will end badly. Your end will be better, and you are going to be very happy.

The disappointments in your past do not mean that the future will be also filled with disappointments. There is still a great chance of things getting better. There are a lot of possibilities to achieve something positive. You aren't going to stay small forever – you are going to go big, so be happy about that. Be happy about the fact that your future is going to be brighter, and the things you have been through are going to be over very soon because you are going to reach a new height.

Be happy because your future is brighter. Look forward to a brighter day and fix your eyes on the new things that are about to occur in your life. The old things have passed, and all things are new. You are about to discover the beauty that lies inside you. The world is about to know that you are very precious. People will celebrate you from every nation and tribe. You are going to see that your life is worth a lot more, and money can never buy the happiness that life is about to give to you.

Stop thinking about what has happened to you. Instead, start thinking of what you can make happen. If you focus on the bad things that have happened to you in the past, you aren't going to be happy. I want you to be happy. Don't you know that you are very special and blessed? You have a lot of talents and gifts, and you are going to use them to make things happen. Focus on that and keep your mind on the things that you are about to do. Be glad and excited because you are about to do new things that will turn around your life.

There is a lot you can do to make a difference in the world. You can be the first to invent something. You can have a great idea and implement it so that it will be useful to others. You don't have to be a victim of your circumstances; you do not have to fill your memory with bad circumstances. You are going to make a big difference in this world and change the lives of many. You are going to transfer something wonderful to the lives of others. Be happy about what you are about to do and the fact that the world is going to know you.

In order to be happy, you can set new goals and come up with a new you. Draw a new plan for your life; write down things that make you excited. Focus on the things that make you happy and keep you feeling strong. Think about new ideas that you can implement into your life, and look for ways in which you can make things better. Upgrade yourself and be very modern. By doing so, you will be happy and competent.

In order to be happy, you have to know that you can always move on and even go further than others who think they are better than you. You can go to places you haven't been to before. You can make progress by updating every area of your life. You can build something brighter for yourself. You can build better relationships and keep your connection strong with those that make you happy. You can move on to more effective uses for your talents and gifts.

You do not have to be sad; there is a lot of happiness that your new actions can create for your future. You don't have to remain depressed. Why should you feel down and think everything is over? Your greatness is going to shine in this world, and as long as you believe that, you will feel very happy. Make plans to take new actions that will bring happiness to your life. You can become the happiest person in this world by taking just one step.

Do not stay with people that do not appreciate the new things that you want to do. Don't stay with people that do not have time for your greatness. You need the right people who will show a sign of appreciation and a sense of being pleased about how you want to make new things happen. If people aren't happy for you, then they can leave. Be happy with yourself and keep around the people that cheer you up.

I understand that you might not be happy with where you are at the moment. Maybe you are thinking of taking some risks. In life, you can never avoid risks, but you still have to believe that something will work out. You should be happy with the outcome of the risks you have taken; even if the outcome is not as perfect as you wish, be happy anyway. Not all your investments will fail; one or two will still work out. You have to hope that some good results will happen. You are better off having a mix of things to do than to having nothing to do at all. Be happy wherever you are and don't let anything stop your happiness. The fact that you are trying something is great, and you should be happy about it. When you try in life, it's a great effort, and you should be happy about it. Your happiness should not depend on what people say to you – it should depend on your affirmations to yourself. Always give yourself words of affirmation even when things do not work out right. Stand strong and keep your happiness even when the day does not go as you expected. Be a surprise source of happiness in this world and maintain your happiness; let it shine.

Positive affirmations can make you happy. Positive affirmations are words that you say to yourself to make you feel positive and perfect. Use positive affirmations towards yourself, such as, 'My circumstances do not create me; I create my circumstances.' Every day when you wake up, pronounce something good into your life. Make a bold declaration of what you want to become. Bless yourself first, even before blessing other people. Understanding and applying positive affirmations will make you grow into a happy person.

You can live in the moment like there is no tomorrow. This means you can maximise how you live your life. You can give the moment the best and achieve the highest possible level of happiness. Various things you can do to live in the moment include dancing like nobody's watching, taking notice of the world, focusing on whatever you are doing, smiling when you wake up, committing acts of kindness, complimenting someone, and making the world a better place. These activities will place you in a positive mood and will increase your happiness.

You should always have something to look forward to; this will keep you happy and encouraged. Make plans that are exciting and think of exciting things to do. Remember the lovely things that you have done in the past, and do them again. Do the things that make you have a good time. Connect with people that make you think positively about yourself. Make plans to possess great things. Think about how you can obtain the best out of the places you go.

Recently, I have seen people that follow their gut, and they end up been happier than people that do not. Always follow your instinct, even if you are in the midst of others. Do not allow people to make decisions for you. Don't let anyone push you to places you do not want to go. Stand for your character, and don't allow others to pollute your mind with evil things. Remember that your nature is important and treasured – don't allow anyone to make you do what you do not want to do.

Look for other ways to be happy, such as making enough money to meet your basic needs, staying close to friends and families, having deep and meaningful conversations, and finding happiness in the job you have. Make room for happiness in your life wherever you are. You can do things that make you laugh. Laughing is a good ingredient of happiness and can also help you to forget pain.

Always say what you mean and mean what you say. Speak from your heart and let the people around you know what is in your heart. Share with them how you feel if you aren't happy about something they have done; by doing so, you can solve the problem instead of keeping pain on the inside. Be positively assertive, because the purpose of life is happiness. Be determined to live a transparent life whereby people can view you as a genuine person. By doing so, you will be very happy.

Your happiness leads to self-celebration. Gain your happiness today and discover that you are not in this world to live a sad life. There is nothing wrong with you being happy and bubbly. If you are not happy, then something is wrong. Make sure you do not leave your happiness outside the door. Always draw happiness to yourself. Be proud of your happiness and allow others to see it. Prove that you are a happy person.

Avoid idleness. By doing the smallest thing you can, you will be filled with self-celebration.

Chapter 25
Idleness

Always find at least one thing to do every day, from typing on a computer to visiting a friend. If you are idle, you will not be able to celebrate yourself. Idleness will not enable you to see the value of yourself. No matter how small it is, find something purposeful to do. You don't have to do something big every time, because the little things go a long way. Anytime you try, you deserve praise.

Idleness can make you feel like you are not important. Instead of being idle, try to use the gifts and talents that you have. Take a step and exercise the good things that are inside of you by engaging in a meaningful activity. Bring into play the greatness that lies inside you. Apply your know-how in making things happen. Use your gifts and talents to make things happen.

Don't spend your time on idleness – spend it on a quality project. Anytime you get active, there is a reward for it.

Do something that you enjoy, and have some fun while you are active. Occupy your mind with something new and amazing. Don't allow time to pass you by without you having something to say that you have done. Don't let your gifts and talents lie empty. Always make a move and do something in order to celebrate yourself.

You are not lazy, and so do not allow anyone to call you lazy. If they do, do not believe them. Sometimes you need a rest, and you do not have to be active. However, make sure that you always have something to do each day. Get your friends together and do something great with them. Go to various places and have fun. Visit locations you have not been before. Remember the things that you enjoy when you are active, and apply them to your life to do something wonderful.

Whenever you see people doing things, get involved and show your talent. Do not sit there feeling like you aren't qualified to do the same things. You may be even better than those who are already doing it. You can shake off your shyness and use your activeness to bring happiness into your life. There is a lot that you can do. You can enjoy your day by doing something great.

You deserve a lively and happy life. You can use your energy in positive ways to produce something that will make others celebrate you. You can rise and do beautiful things. Anything you touch should come out as a beautiful thing. You should touch things and leave them with a beautiful finish. You can be very lively and dynamic in a way that Others will respect you for it.

Instead of being idle, go ahead of others in every journey in your life. Make things happen and plan for your future. Take actions that will bring greatness into your life. Promise yourself that you will never give up until you receive a change. Make sure that you keep going and that you respect the fact that you are a very special person who deserves something awesome.

If you have been idle in the past, it's time for you to discover the gifts and talents inside you. You have qualities that you can use to do something awesome. You can start now by taking a step, no matter how small it is. It will never be part of your life history that you are someone who did not know the gifts and talents you have. You have a lot of talents on the inside, so start using them. Make that little effort to bring a shining light into your life.

You can become someone that will be in demand. When you start developing the gifts and talents, you will see that people will need you everywhere. They will always want to be with you and will want to mix with you. They will want to learn your secrets and will want you to be a role model in their lives. You can be on top, and you can become the choice of the nation today.

You can start getting involved with activities that will help you explore life. By exploring life, you will see that it is very interesting and is not a boring place at all. You will see that life can be very enjoyable and filled with glory. It can lead you to a place where you will always be celebrated, and you will feel like a king or a queen. You aren't in this life by mistake – you have been counted to be part of this life, and your days are going to be glowing.

If you are someone that spends most of the time being busy and hardworking, that's good for you. I want you to know that your hard work is not going to be in vain; it will bring fruits into your life. It will take you to a great place in life where people will know you. Your hard work of today is going to benefit you in your future. Keep being diligent in your life. Keep doing thorough work in your workplace, with your children, in your personal life, and in your marriage. You will see that the future will be very bright for you. It's going to pay off. The thorough work you are doing is going to cause you to shine, and no one is going to stop you. You are going to see that the careful work you have done is going to brighten your life and put you on top.

If you are idle, you will not be able to celebrate yourself. In order for someone to celebrate himself, he has to have something that he is doing. Laying your hands upon something, no matter how small, will give you a great opportunity to have something to celebrate. I hear you saying, 'Oh, I do not have a great gift or talent.' Just use your talent as it is. Even the smallest talents will give you a greater focus and target, bringing joy into your life. There is nothing that is too small. All you have is greatness. You are not small at all. You are going to win. One day you are going to become a successful story that will surprise others. You are going to discover how special you are, and you will become someone big tomorrow. You are going to overcome your challenges and step out in a new way. You will see that the way you have been busy today will lead you to catch something better than you had in your past.

By not living idly, you will see that you are full of life and energy. You will be able to see yourself come out as the best. You will have lots of opportunity into which you can tap. You will have a variety of chances to do something you like. You will be head to places that interest you, and you will discover yourself more as you spend time in the midst of people. You'll see the picture of yourself clearer and discover that you are very capable.

When someone isn't idle, that person is functioning. By functioning, you will be able to present yourself in the presence of people, and you will see them show their appreciation to you for your good deeds. They will love to be with you and will show you how great you are. They can see the work of your hands and will be a witness of your talent, testifying about how you behave and treat people well. Then, you will have lots of things to celebrate.

Someone can be idle because she has some health problems that are stopping her from functioning, and I do understand that. I know that health problems can get in the way of functioning like one did in the past. However, you are still a wonderful person, and there is still a lot of greatness on the inside of you. Do whatever little thing you can do to keep yourself busy. You do not have to be like others. Love yourself despite your condition, knowing that one day your health will get better and you will be able to do lots of things. If you believe in God, believe that he will heal you.

Always do things what makes you feel enthusiastic every day. Don't keep busy for the sake of it — make sure that what you are doing falls in line with your dreams, talents, gifts, and qualities. Do what you love doing, and go for things that follow up with your inner expectations. You do not have to copy others, because you have the right to be unique. Do things about which you are passionate; do things that your whole heart wants to do.

Idleness can make you bored and make you lose your purpose. I am not saying that you cannot spend some time relaxing or meditating during each day; rest is important, and you need that rest. You also need some time to chill out and cool off, which protects your mental state. However, if you are bored, you will not be able to give an account of what you have done during the day. Idleness can make you form bad habits. When you are idle, you are likely to pick up some non-useful habits and addictions which can be dangerous to your health. You might also start doing things that does not add glory to your life. Try to keep yourself busy to protect yourself from falling for things that are not necessary. As you keep yourself busy, you will be able to achieve something about which you will feel special. Don't worry about your imperfections – just try to do whatever you can, and that is enough.

Idleness can make you waste time, and time is very valuable. You need time to get things done. Time waits for no man, and you shouldn't just let time go without producing something special. The time you can spend creating something new or taking great actions will be lost if you are idle. You have to occupy yourself with something so that at the end of the day, you can remember what you have been able to achieve, which will be great for you.

Idle hands are the devil's workshop. If you are idle, people can start using you for purposes that makes no sense. You might start mixing with bad friends; you might start going to places that have no use for your destiny. People can use you for their own selfish benefits when you are idle; they have nothing to give you in return, but they want to use you to solve their problems. You are not made for that. Idleness can make you start thinking of negative things, which can lead to negative actions.

If you do not want your mind to be occupied with negative things, then make sure you aren't idle. A negative mind is not healthy and does not befit your destiny. A negative mind happens when you are idle, and it can make you lose the perfect picture of who you really are on the inside. You need a healthy mind in order to enjoy your life and see yourself as the best. You can even choose to keep a friend around so that your mind can have something positive to ponder. Do not remain alone.

Some people get idle because they are waiting for others to do things. I know that you are not perfect, but there are still capabilities inside you. I know that sometimes you can be shy about doing something, perhaps because of the people around or a large crowd. Maybe you are thinking that people are going to judge you. Don't let that stop you! Remember that others' judgement cannot stop you from dreaming on the inside. Try not to leave things for other people to do – participate yourself, and no matter how small your effort is, you will be able to look back and say that you have done something and had fun while doing it.

Some people become idle because they believe they don't deserve something. Maybe you feel you do not deserve to be among those that are doing a specific project. I want you to know that you are very special, and people are waiting for you to get things done. You do not know how amazing you are until you try. Do not look down on yourself, because those that are doing it are humans like you; they are not better than you, and neither are they more capable than you. They are likely to make mistakes, too.

Maybe instead of you doing things, you try and rely on others. Sometimes we rely on other people's power; we feel they are better and stronger. People like to depend on the intelligence of others, feeling their own intelligence will not be good enough to solve the problems. You are very intelligent and fully capable, to the extent that you will produce fine results when you lay your hands on something. You are very special.

Idleness can cause you to have a low level of productivity. If you spend most of your time being idle, you will produce less. If you feel that you have been idle throughout the day, start spending your time doing something. Even window shopping will keep you busy. Simply do something you enjoy or something that is of interest to you, from writing a book to going for a dance lesson. Occupy yourself with something that will help you view your productivity. You will yield a lot when you keep yourself busy.

Look for someone who will listen to you and who will give you something to celebrate.

Chapter 26
Going to Non-Listeners

In life, you need people who will listen to you. You deserve to be listened to and understood. Do not take your problems to people who do not listen to you. Listening is the ability to keep quiet while hearing others speak. Listening is the ability to accept what someone has said without offering advice or judging. If the people in your life are not listening to you, I hope that you will meet people that will listen to you tomorrow. I know what it feels like when you tell someone your problem, and the person doesn't seem to listen. It makes you feel like no one cares and leaves you with a sense of incompleteness. You want someone who understands, and that is what matters. You want someone that will agree with you. You need someone who will say yes when you say yes and will say no when you say no. You need someone who will say it as you want it to be said, who will agree with what is inside your heart.

If the people in your life do not show you tender love

when you share your problems with them, I can assure you that one day you will find someone who will. There is someone out there who is very good at listening to people; that sort of person is ready to be your friend and build a close relationship with you. If the people in your life are currently giving you advice and showing you how you should do things right – instead of listening to you and showing you tender love – then you will soon find a better person who will be there for you as you expect.

I personally have certain issues in my life whereby I am looking for someone who will listen to and understand me. I am looking for someone who will say, 'um' while I am talking and will agree with what I am saying. I want someone who feels what I am going through, someone who will defend me and not say negative things to me. I am not really looking for advice; I am only looking for someone who will understand me. I also need that person to support me. Most of the people in my life do not have that characteristics, but I finally found someone whom I can trust in that aspect.

You need people that can pay attention to you, take notice of the good things you do, and uplift you because of them. You need people who are able to cover your faults and place attention on your glory and beauty. You need people who will encourage you and keep you going. You need people who will concentrate on the possibilities that lie inside of you, and who will have a creative thought about your future and the gifts and talents you possess.

The listener in your life should be aware of your capabilities, qualities, strength, gifts, and talents. He should see you in a different way from how the world sees you, and he should hold a precious place in your heart. Your listener will consider you to be right even when the majority feels you are wrong. Your listener is someone to whom you find it easy to talk. He will treat you in a special way and will view you as an awesome person. The listener will take note of your ability to survive and win despite the tough wind that is blowing on your life. Your listener will always give you hope and something to look forward to. He will view you as an exceptional person, even in the days where you feel down and pessimistic about your achievements.

Your listener will believe in what you do and will see you as a distinctive person, celebrating every moment of your life with you. He will make you joyful and happy even when it looks like nothing is working out. Your listener will make you feel like you are better than others. Your listener will see you as very intelligent and capable, even if there are still some little areas in which you need improvement.

You will always flow in conversation with your listener. You will be able to run to him anytime you feel like sharing something. You will be able to pour your heart out and share things. You can share your current problems or issues with your listener so that he can be updated about what is going on in your life. Your listener will always check on you so that he can know how you feel and how things are.

You will be very proud of yourself when you meet people that are able to listen to you. No matter how perfect you are, you will have some weaknesses, bad times, and negative situations, you may wish to share them. You want the person you will share them with to listen to you. You don't want the person to turn a deaf ear. You want him to accept what you are saying, feel for you, show some pity, and maybe give you a hug.

Some situations we face are like being put into the fire. This is when a listener is important. You don't really need advice in the fire; instead, you need someone that can encourage you. Your listener should be there for you and help you to believe in yourself. He should give you hope and help you see a way out. A good listener is someone who is able to give you affirmations when you are stuck or are feeling down. When you take a problem to your listener, he will be able to tell you things like, 'You are a winner, and you are going to succeed. Your problem will be over soon.' The words of your listener should bring healing to your life, giving you strength during your tough days. When you take a problem to a non-listener, your mind will be left in a bad situation. The words of the non-listener will play in your mind, and you will be left with doubt. Listeners are people that are mature and caring.

Sometimes you will find people that are natural listeners; it's simply their nature to listen to you. Listeners are also positive people; they are not ready to judge others. They will listen to the bad or good experiences you are willing to share. They will present good body language as part of their reaction to what you are saying. We do not like it when people pass judgement on us; we want to be received and treated right, no matter the experience. Therefore be sensitive to people that are helpful and kind towards you when you share your problems. We want the people who have listened to us to keep valuing us. We do not want to be treated differently from others because we have shared our problems. In your life, keep your listeners well and always thank them. Your listener will show some sign of respect towards you and will carry you up as someone that is worthy. The listener will not use his words to bring you down.

As a person, I have been through terrible situations, and despite my positivity, I have said things that looked negative. I was trying to share what I was going through with my listener. Life is not easy, and sometimes you need someone who will hold you up when you are feeling down, who will always back you up even when you are falling. You need someone on whom you can always rely. There was a way that I felt, and I wanted the person whom I was sharing it with to know my feelings. I was not happy in a situation, and because I was unable to get rid of it, I was looking for someone that would understand me.

You might be looking for someone that will understand you, and the characteristics of those you have spoken to in the past might make you feel you can never find anyone better. That's a lie – you don't have to believe that. The words of a good listener will always make you feel good, like you are the most precious person in the world. He will make you feel very special even on days when there are lots of things going wrong in your life. The words of a good listener will help you to sense positive things about yourself and the things you do.

On the other hand, it can be difficult to find someone who will listen to the good experiences you want to share. Sometimes your heart can be filled with joy about something, and you are looking for someone who can feel the way you feel. You want others to be as happy as you are; you want them to shout and feel great about the experience you shared with them. You can't share it with yourself, but one day you will find a friend in this world who will see things the way you do and will jump for joy as you do. That someone will be glad and will rejoice about your good news.

However, you should still rejoice on your own if you cannot get someone to rejoice with you. Never stop rejoicing. You should never give up. You know what your life is worth, and you do not have to feel bad when it seems there is no one rejoicing with you. Believe in yourself and see yourself as someone who is going far in life. View yourself as great, and celebrate that fact.

Listeners are a blessing to our lives because of the way they listen to us and show that they care. We all want someone to listen to us, and anytime they do we feel touched and blessed. I believe that you will find a good listener who will be able to give up himself, listen to you, truly understand you, and be on your side.

Listeners are people whom we value because they treat us with a high value and do not look down on us. They still love us despite our little faults, and they do not share with others what we have told them. Anytime we feel like talking, we can go to them. Be happy about the listeners in your life, and always keep the precious things you want to say for them. Say it to them and allow them to give you the kind of feedback you expect.

I am sure you don't want to take your issues to non-listeners, because that can steal your joy. Non-listeners can be very degrading, and most of them are people who do not love themselves. Someone who does not love himself cannot love you; the only love he can show to you is the one he has shown himself. It's like a hungry man feeding hungry people: he has to feed himself first before he has the strength to feed others. Instead, go to someone who will listen to you and tell you how great and strong you are in the midst of your challenges.

It is very difficult when you live with family members who do not listen to you. You want your family members to always listen to you and respond positively to what you say. Maybe you aren't happy about something they are doing towards you. I want you to still keep your joy in the midst of that. Believe in who you are and see yourself as someone who will go far in life. I want you to know that one day you will find someone who listens and cares.

If you are expecting people to change because they are

not listening to you, realise that it is very hard to change people. Do not expect yourself to change them. I hope that they will change for your benefit, but if they do not, you can't force them. They will change if they want to and if they realise why they need to change. That's why sometimes it is good for us to mind our own business and not get into other people's personal lives. If you are with a difficult person, look for ways to keep yourself happy so that their actions will not affect you negatively.

If someone is doing something that is affecting you in a bad way, you don't have to keep waiting and expecting them to change. Leave them to carry on with their lives. Live your own life well, enjoy your days, and satisfy yourself. Live for your dreams and aspire for something different and great in life. Keep your smile on, cheer yourself up when you are down, dream big, make yourself proud, celebrate yourself, and have a wonderful life.

If what others are doing is affecting you negatively, then you can expect some changes from them, because by doing so you are making your life better. However, do not be hard on others if they aren't doing something that is affecting you negatively. If what they are doing is truly affecting you negatively, then you need to boldly face them with the situation. You have to speak out and let them know the truth. You must stand your ground and give them some warning, or report the issue to the appropriate authority.

If you want someone who can listen and also give you advice, look within your friends and highlight the one that possesses that characteristic. Look for the advice you want in the right places, and get it from someone who can tell you the truth or lead you to the right place. Receive advice from a friend you trust or who you feel is capable of giving you the right information.

There is no limit to your ability to have friends. You can always make new friends in your local library, church, shops, school, or workplace. You can exchange phone numbers with people. You can open up and get to know them by conversing with them on the phone or by meeting up with them once in a while. You will see that there are people out there who are willing to give you the best and see you become what you want to become in life.

Listeners are people who give you attention and also place their attention on your destiny. They do not want you to fall down or make a mistake. They are careful to lead you right and give you guidance when you need it. They are not harsh towards you and do not throw just any word at you. I would not really call them advisers, because the job of a listener is not to advise. Listeners carefully listen and are very gentle with their attitude towards you.

Listeners are people who want your future to be bright. They are very careful not to speak anything negative into your life. They are always caring towards you, and they give you attention. They care about your feelings and can see your talents and gifts. They remind you of how brilliant you are and help your mind get a better picture of who you really are. They motivate you to climb higher in life, and you will see yourself achieve more because of them.

When we talk to people, we expect something out of it. It might be a laugh, silence, a response, or an action. If we do not receive what we expect, we are likely to not talk to them anymore. If the people you are talking to are not fulfilling your expectations, that means something is missing. That missing thing might make you feel weak and a bit let down. However, don't give up on getting to know new people who can fulfil your expectations.

A good listener does not want you to experience bad things in life and will not go to others to share your personal issues. A listener will tell you that you will be okay and will always remind you about how bright your future is. When you meet good listeners, cling to them and let them know that you need them. Love them to bits and take time to connect with them. Allow them to pour their love on you, and let them use their gift of listening to be a blessing in your life. Let them transform your mind and fill it with wonders.

You can always put your confidence in listeners. Even when you fall, they are ready to pick you up. No matter the hell that you go through, they will still be there for you, and you can always trust them. They will remind you of how excellent you are and will hold you up with pride. They will always speak good things about you, and they will take good care of you. You will be well looked after in the hands of listeners. They will treat you well and show you that you always have to value yourself.

Conclusion

I believe you are now ready to celebrate yourself. I believe you have gained a better way of viewing you. I know you have dreams and you now understand why it is going to come through. This book should open your eyes to see new opportunities to grow in life. You should now have words of comfort for every problem you may be going through. You are not alone. You are special.

There is a desire on the inside of you. You have to discover your inner desires because it forms your life and your future. You desire to become someone or something in life. I am here to announce to you that the desire cannot die. It will fulfil its purpose. You are going to achieve certain things in your life through your desire. You will give birth to every dream you are carrying. You will be lifted in this life.

You will be restored of the things that you have lost. The issues in your life will be settled. You are going to get better. Your past mistakes are no more hindrances to your glorious future. Using this book, you should discover your gifts, talents, interests, abilities, skills, desires and purpose. You should see clearly now the position you desire in life and have plans of how you will get there.

Sometimes people, life or situations can do you evil but always remember that it will only turn out for your good at the end. You will be a winner and a strong individual. Things will work out to your advantage. You are a good person and you will enjoy the finest things in life.

This book will help you discover who you are. You will discover your talents, gifts, abilities, skills, desires and purpose. When you discover who you are, you will not live according to the way people, your past, your bad habits and external circumstances define you. You will no longer be controlled by people. Life will not happen to you but you will happen to life, meaning you will always be shining in the midst of life's storm. You will survive in life.

Fear, worry and negative thinking is not your portion. You are more than a conqueror. Your future has amazing things in store for you. You are going to receive every good thing that you have been expecting. Keep up the good work you are doing and at the end you will smile and be filled with great joy.

Fear and faith have something in common. Both wants you

to believe something will happen. However, fear wants you to believe that something bad will happen while faith wants you to believe that something good will happen. Fear will tell you that you are not going to be happy again while faith tells you that good things are in store for you. You have to stand strong against the fear and pick up the faith. Use the faith to your advantage and start producing great things.

You can now relax and be very patient through the experiences you go through in life because you know there are rewards waiting ahead of you. Things are going to get better and your life will receive a change. Your time is coming and you also will win and have testimonies about your life. Keep this book as a treasure because it will help you in all that you go through.